THE ROYAL AIR FORCE BENEVOLENT FUND'S

# INTERNATIONAL AIR TATTOO

## SILVER JUBILEE 1971-1996

IMPERIAL TOBACCO was proud to sponsor the first International Air Tattoo in 1971 and is delighted at being given the honour of supporting the production of this anniversary publication to celebrate its Silver Jubilee.

IMPERIAL TOBACCO LIMITED

# INTERNATIONAL AIR TATTOO SILVER JUBILEE 1971-1996

Published by

**The Royal Air Force Benevolent Fund Enterprises Publications Unit**,
Building 15, RAF Fairford, Glos GL7 4DL, England

Publishing Director:
**Paul A. Bowen**

Publishing Co-ordinator:
**Karen Pell**

Compiled and Edited:
**Peter R. March**
Contributing Authors:
**Jack Currie, Ben Dunnell and William R. Newby-Grant**
RIAT Checklist:
**Ben Dunnell**
Emblems, badges and stickers:
**Robby Robinson**

Photography:
The International Air Tattoo Team: **Gordon Bartley (GB), Ben Dunnell (BD), John Dunnell (JD), Graham Finch (GF), Andrew March (APM), Daniel March (DJM), Peter R March (PRM), Brian Strickland (BSS)** and as credited. We are indebted to the many supporters of The Royal International Air Tattoo who took the trouble to send their photographs for consideration – their names appear with the photographs that have been included.

Design: **Graham Finch Design**
Cover artwork: **Wilfred Hardy GAvA**

ISBN 1 899808 70 1

PRINTED IN HONG KONG

THE ROYAL AIR FORCE BENEVOLENT FUND'S

# INTERNATIONAL AIR TATTOO SILVER JUBILEE 1971-1996

# CONTENTS

# INTRODUCTION

Imperial Tobacco has been one of this country's leading sponsors for over 30 years and in 1971 we were given the honour of supporting the first Embassy Air Tattoo which was held at RAF Greenham Common.

It is, therefore, most fitting that Imperial Tobacco should join in the 25th Anniversary celebrations by sponsoring the production of this anthology, which charts the progress of the International Air Tattoo during those 25 years.

The popularity of the Tattoo remains undiminished and, quite rightly, retains its pre-eminence as the most spectacular air show in the world - providing not only superb entertainment for its many thousands of spectators, but also contributing towards the necessary finance which enables the Royal Air Force Benevolent Fund to carry out its vital work in the service of others. The granting of Royal status to the International Air Tattoo earlier this year was a much deserved acclamation and provided yet another milestone for all those who have been involved over the years.

During the years since 1971, Imperial has maintained its association by supporting many of the events and activities arranged by The Royal International Air Tattoo. In 1985, support from Imperial Tobacco enabled the Fund to provide flying displays by G-HUEY, a Bell UH-1 helicopter captured during the Falklands conflict: and the Superkings Trophy for the best solo jet display has been a regular feature at all of the Air Tattoos since 1985.

The hugely successful concert tours by the Massed Bands of the Royal Air Force started in 1987 with a gala concert at the Royal Albert Hall, and such has been their popularity that, during this year's tour, the Bands will perform at twelve concert halls throughout the United Kingdom.

Our long tradition of support for the Fund is one in which we take great pride. Sponsorship of these concerts helps to provide the much-needed resources which help the Fund to continue its vital work. It also ensures that the Massed Bands of the RAF and their music can be enjoyed by many thousands of people, giving them the opportunity to support the Fund whilst deriving great pleasure from the live performances of these fine musicians; and I am delighted that Imperial Tobacco's support for the concert tour will continue into the next millennium.

This commemoration, in words and pictures, will evoke many happy memories of The Royal International Air Tattoo for the thousands of airmen, airwomen and civilian personnel who have contributed towards its phenomenal success, whilst also providing a lasting reminder of the thrills and excitement the Tattoos have brought to so many people during the last 25 years.

*Gareth Davis*

**Gareth Davis**
Chief Executive
Imperial Group Plc

# FOREWORD

## by Air Marshal Sir Denis Crowley-Milling
### KCB CBE DSO DFC* AE RAF

I took over as Controller of the Royal Air Force Benevolent Fund in 1975. At that time, as it still does, the Fund managed a number of Trusts – and one of my first jobs was to examine their potential benefits. Almost immediately I discovered the Fund's Development Trust.

It had arisen from the Royal Air Force Display at Farnborough in 1950, the Service's first post-war airshow to raise money for the Benevolent Fund and an attempt to recreate Hendon's golden days of the 1920s and 1930s. Although the event successfully raised a substantial sum, Britain was then struggling to recover from one conflict whilst at the same time making a stand with her allies in the Cold War. A stretched RAF and depressed economy probably combined to put a temporary end to the large public airshow. Whatever the precise reasons the Farnborough money, donated to the Fund by the Air Force Board and designated for the financing of future airshows, had lain unused for 25 years.

On hearing of this, Air Commodore John McKelvey, my Secretary of Appeals, suggested that the climate might then be right to reinstate the Fund's tradition of airshows – first conceived by Lord Trenchard in 1920, in the face of the hardship suffered by wounded Great War airmen and bereaved families, and influential opposition to an independent air force. It was an idea which appealed to me. John McKelvey was already in touch with the organisers of the 'Embassy Air Tattoo', staged since 1971 to raise money for RAF Charities. They were developing an interesting track record, so we asked them to come to see us.

Tattoo Director Paul Bowen and its Director of Flying, Tim Prince (both civil air traffic controllers in 'real' life) arrived with the entire team, including the press officer on crutches, leaving my substantial, old-fashioned conference table without a seat to spare. They were very persuasive with an enthusiasm which proved to be infectious. We decided to back them, financed by the Development Trust, and to run the Fund's first modern airshow at RAF Greenham Common in July 1976.

It was perhaps a natural choice that I should invite my former war-time leader Group Captain Douglas Bader to become President of what was now to be called 'International Air Tattoo'. With Sir Douglas Bader as the President and figurehead of the IAT team and myself as Chairman, IAT blossomed into the premier air display and eventually the largest of its kind in the world. But from the start a safe airshow was paramount to all of us, and my major concern.

For the early airshows the set-up was certainly somewhat primitive by today's standards. But over the years there are some things which have never changed – the commitment and energy of the ever-growing team of splendid volunteers who help to run IAT, a dedication to the safety and enjoyment of our spectators,

**HRH The Duke of Kent, Sir Douglas Bader and Air Marshal Sir Denis Crowley-Milling at Greenham Common.**

**Paul Bowen (left) and Tim Prince (right) join Sir Denis in cutting the 25th anniversary cake at The Royal International Air Tattoo.** Richard Wintle

and the aim of meeting Trenchard's mandate of promoting the Royal Air Force and raising money for the Fund's much needed welfare work. I am indeed proud to have been part of it, from the modest beginnings to all the 20 years of success that have followed.

I would very much like to thank Imperial Tobacco Limited for generously supporting this colourful record of the past 25 years of IAT and this year's magnificent Royal International Air Tattoo.

*Air Marshal Sir Denis Crowley Milling KCB CBE DSO DFC* AE RAF was Chairman of International Air Tattoo from 1976-1981 and has been Vice-Patron since 1983. He was Controller of the Royal Air Force Benevolent Fund from 1975-1981.*

# PREFACE

Having been involved as a volunteer in every Air Tattoo and all of the 'in between' events since 1971, I feel well qualified to compile this special 25th anniversary review. Like many of the volunteer managers I have been called upon to do a number of jobs - photographer, press & public relations officer, programme editor, media reporter and airshow researcher during the 25 years. From the very first encounter with Paul Bowen, his late father Pat, Tim Prince and Jack Currie at North Weald, I was drawn to their single-minded determination and enthusiasm for the development of a unique organisation for the presentation of what was quickly to become the finest military airshow in the world.

It was never easy or straightforward, as there always seemed to be unexpected obstacles and problems. The air tattoo location was often in jeopardy. North Weald had a decaying infrastructure and the M11 motorway was planned to cross the edge of the airfield. Greenham Common had the proximity of Aldermaston to cope with, and then there was the emergency use for Ugandan Asians, the arrival of the Cruise missiles and the notorious 'peace camp'. While the early shows were under the aegis of RAFA South East, there was an uneasy relationship with the area management that culminated in the resignation of Jack Currie and a crisis meeting of the volunteer managers.

I well remember that it was held at a public house in Wiltshire where a small group of us decided to support Paul and Tim with a future airshow if they could come up with a new organisation for the air tattoo to work under, and a formula that would bring in new sponsors and keep our original sponsors Imperial Tobacco on board.

A great deal of the early shows' success was down to this company's financial support. Within a short space of time the two airshow enthusiasts were back telling us that IAT 76 would be taking place at Greenham Common under the auspices of the RAF Benevolent Fund and a major commercial sponsor would be helping to underwrite the event.

Like myself, many of the people in the management of the Air Tattoos are civilians with no direct service background nor in many cases professionally involved in aviation, yet they have worked together with men and women from all three services to present a unique military airshow. This has called for a great deal of tact and understanding from every quarter.

The inspiration and leadership for this has come through the Controllers of the RAF Benevolent Fund and their Board members. Air Marshal Sir Denis Crowley Milling and Sir Douglas Bader together lifted the IAT volunteers from a rather depressed and disorganised state back into the lively and enthusiastic airshow management team with its huge band of volunteers workers. Their work was carried on by Air Chief Marshal Sir Alasdair Steedman and Air Chief Marshal Sir Jock Kennedy, who helped the International Air Tattoo to grow in stature and importance on the world aerospace stage.

IAT has not been without its share of problems. It became an increasingly difficult task to create a large profit from the show for the RAF Benevolent Fund, as costs steadily mounted, without the generous support of an ever widening number of commercial sponsors. The Nationwide Building Society, Lloyds Bank, the Alliance & Leicester Building Society, British Aerospace, Lockheed Martin, SAGA and Rover have been amongst the supporters who have joined with Imperial Tobacco for over two decades. From these large organisations it is not surprising that there have been a number of individuals who have gone out of their way to assist IAT and the Fund. In particular Fred Crawley, the former Chief Executive of Lloyds Bank and Chairman of Alliance & Leicester Building Society and Girobank has, since 1979, played a key part in raising commercial sponsorship. He is now Deputy Chairman of The Royal International Air Tattoo and Treasurer of the RAF Benevolent Fund.

The International Air Tattoo organising team and its many volunteer helpers have today, as they did two decades ago, two major objectives – to present the best and most entertaining military airshow in the world and in so doing raise much needed money for the charitable work of the Royal Air Force Benevolent Fund. If, on the way to achieving this, they get some personal pleasure and satisfaction, it is a bonus.

In 1995 a major step forward came with the eight-hour airshow being presented as 'theatre of the air', divided into different scenes and acts and culminating in the widely acclaimed Victory Salute. IAT is now calling upon the professional skills and talents of its volunteer managers as never before, and where there is a gap, going out to seek out the right person to fill it. The event has grown from a £5000 budget to costing over £2m to put on; its contributions to the RAF Benevolent Fund have risen from a few thousand pounds to a quarter of a million pounds and it attracts world-wide attendance.

The success of IAT can be attributed to many factors, all of which have their roots back in 1971 and the team under the inspired leadership of Jack Currie, that had the foresight and imagination to develop the concept of a major international military airshow, run by a large number of unpaid volunteers working together to raise money for an RAF charity. It is one thing to have the vision, but quite another to carry it through for 25 years and still be enthusiastically developing it.

The credit for this goes to Paul Bowen and Tim Prince, who have steered the air tattoo through all its trials and tribulations to the huge, spectacular airshow that this year became The Royal International Air Tattoo. But they could not have achieved it without the dedication and enormous support from many thousands of IAT managers and volunteers, the personnel of air arms from around the world and the countless agencies and commercial organisations that have freely given their assistance.

This anniversary book through its brief narrative and selection of photographs can only highlight some of the events, personalities and aircraft that have been part of 25 years of air tattoos and associated airshows. The more comprehensive coverage of this year's Royal International Air Tattoo fully illustrates the true picture of the world's greatest military airshow in its silver jubilee year.

**Peter R March**
September 1996

# AIR TATTOO

## THE FIRST 25 YEARS

### The Beginning

During the 1960s, the Royal Air Forces Association's South Eastern Area organised a number of air displays at the former Battle of Britain aerodrome at North Weald in the County of Essex, 17 miles to the northeast of London. These were single day events and held annually on Spring Bank Holiday Monday, being heavily dependent upon assistance from the Royal Air Force which provided aircraft for the flying and static displays as well as air traffic controllers for the tower.

It was at that time that Paul Bowen, who was then an Air Traffic Control Officer Cadet based at Stansted, first became involved in the world of air displays, initially in this capacity, along with the late Brian Peapell, who was then a serving senior NCO in the RAF.

In 1970, Squadron Leader Jack Currie was employed as Registrar of Nottingham College of Further Education, and was, in his own words, 'rather bored' when he happened to see an advertisement for the post of Area Secretary for the South Eastern Area of the Royal Air Forces Association. The idea appealed to the former Bomber Command pilot – part of the job also included the organisation of an annual air display – so, with this in mind, he attended the 1970 event at North Weald as an observer.

These displays were all organised with the aim of creating profits for the Royal Air Forces Association but, because of their limited scope, did not attract a significant income. There was considerable room for improvement, particularly in the fields of traffic management, parking and pleasure flights, and when Jack Currie was appointed to the post of Area Secretary, he decided that a radical change of approach could substantially improve both the image and profits of such an event. In consultation with Paul Bowen, he determined to create a new team of enthusiastic volunteer helpers for the tasks, which did not require professional expertise, while quite rightly insisting that essential services such as catering, ground displays, advertising, public relations and so forth remained firmly in the hands of professionals. Needless to say, professional support also included air traffic control and all ground and emergency services.

Jack Currie, as Organising Secretary, then convened a series of meetings of volunteer helpers with a view to organising the 1971 Show. This team included Paul Bowen's father, Pat Bowen, and a number of friends including Richard Holmes, *Chalky* White, Christopher and Olaf Hammerbeck, and Bill Newby-Grant, who was approached because of his linguistic knowledge to organise the reception of visiting foreign aircrew, for, as a new departure, participation from abroad was invited. To the team of helpers who met in the conference room of St Margaret's Hospital in Epping, the whole prospect was thoroughly exciting and the enthusiasm of those present was quietly channelled under the genial leadership of the Organising Secretary. Managers were appointed for the apron, public relations, the arena, trade and static displays and they set about recruiting like-minded helpers; thus the strength of the organisation lay in the fact that its members could largely be relied upon to work well with each other.

On Monday 31 May 1971, at ten o'clock, North Weald's gates were opened to the public. The aerodrome, then still owned by the Ministry of Defence, was no longer active and thus had to be re-activated for the event. The aim of the show was to provide entertainment for all the family and, as befits a Tattoo, it included arena events, and a ground as well as a flying display. The show was sponsored by the *Daily Express* and was the first challenge to which Jack Currie's team had been put. Paul Bowen had built up the aerodrome control organisation, receiving considerable help from the staff of the

Ray Hanna taking-off in Spitfire IX MH434 at the first Air Tattoo in 1971. PRM

Aeroplane and Armament Experimental Establishment at Boscombe Down, including the Operations Officer, Tim Prince.

The public came in force. At two o'clock the flying display began with the spectacle of the season's first Formula One Air Race for the *Duke of Edinburgh Trophy*; sadly one of the competitors was to lose his life when the Owl Racer G-AYMS crashed into the River Thames whilst returning to its home base after the show. Jack Currie had insisted on a first-class commentator, John Blake, and in the next few hours a veritable air pageant was to unfold. There was strong Royal Air Force participation in the form of current aircraft, which included Lightning F1A, Nimrod MR1, Belfast C1, Phantom FGR2, and the RAF's mirror-formation team of Jet Provost T5s, the *Gemini Pair*. To recall the past, there was the *Battle of Britain Memorial Flight* and Spitfire LFIXC MH434, then owned by Sir Adrian Swire but, just like today, flown inimitably by Ray Hanna.

5

Among visitors from abroad were numbered the Austrian Air Force, which was delighted to send a Sikorsky S-65OE helicopter in answer to what proved to be its first invitation to fly abroad and thereby forged enduring links with the Air Tattoo. Four Saab A35XD Drakens came from the Royal Danish Air Force to make another first-time appearance in the UK. Particularly welcome were the pilots of two Northrop F-5As from 332 Skvadron of the Royal Norwegian Air Force, which had been formed at North Weald in 1942 and whose squadron insignia was a blue axe. Captain Chris Steensby was accompanied by Lieutenant Joff Oppsal, whose short stature was compensated by the use of a cushion on his ejector seat. No doubt he will long remember this display, as his wedding plans were somewhat disrupted when his aircraft went unserviceable at Leuchars while returning to Norway after the end of the show. The Royal Netherlands Air Force sent an NF-5B, and a flypast by four F-4D Phantoms from the 81st Tactical Fighter Wing of the United States Air Force at RAF Bentwaters supplied American support, which was also to grow with the passing years. The French Air Force provided an immaculate display of teamwork – including a slow roll in mirror formation – by the Fouga CM170 Magisters of *La Patrouille de France*, led by Capitaine Pages who was, sadly, to lose his life shortly afterwards.

The display had its lighter side to alleviate the strain on the organisers. During a spirited simulated ground attack flown by the pilots of the *Gemini Pair*, and while the assault by the Royal Anglian Regiment supported by the Royal Armoured Corps Parachute Squadron went on Ferret armoured cars went in, and the controller of the ground explosions was seen smouldering gently and shaking his fists as he emerged from his straw-bale command post.

Events on the ground were not neglected either: equestrian and motor cycle display teams from the Royal Military Police and Air Training Corps performed in the three-hour arena display. Here also, towards the end of the day, the air race winner received his trophy from

Formula One Owl Racer G-AYMS appeared at North Weald in 1971. PRM

Heavyweight RAF participant at the first Air Tattoo –a Short Belfast . PRM

the Royal Air Forces Associations South Eastern Area President, Air Chief Marshal Sir John Baker and Kenneth More, while at the close The Central Band of The Royal Air Force and the Queen's Colour Squadron, which had previously given a polished performance of continuity drill, performed the Sunset Ceremony.

As the crowd slowly dispersed, the weather-burned organisers began to relax after the tensions of the day and the strains of the weeks

Aircraft from several foreign air arms attended the first Tattoo, including an Austrian Air Force S-65OE (above) and Royal Norwegian Air Force F-5A (top). PRM

*The Blue Eagles* Army Air Corps team flying Sioux helicopters at the '71 show. PRM

The *Patrouille de France* displayed its Fouga Magisters at Air Tattoo '71. PRM

leading up to it. In comparison with later shows it was a small event, but it had provided an insight into the complexities of what lay ahead and had given the various managers practice in the necessary arts of diplomacy and flexibility. The weather had been kind, a large crowd had provided the hitherto unheard of profit of £10,000 for the Royal Air Forces Association and the team welded together under Jack Currie's unobtrusive yet insistent leadership had, all things considered, achieved a success. The new formula show had arrived to replace the old.

By some error, on the following morning, a large group of mass-start racing cyclists had been wrongly informed that they could once more practise on the airfield perimeter track. A little while later the two Norwegian F-5s slid past the control tower – on which the organisers had congregated to wave them and all the other guests farewell – at some speed in the customary way. Their arrival at the edge of the airfield coincided with a gaggle of head-down cyclists who failed to notice their approach, and the person who had originally misinformed the cyclists was actually seen running hard to escape their wrath after they had disentangled themselves from their machines.

## North Weald recalled

There is a raft of memories to choose from, but I will pick one of the earliest, from the 1971 Air Tattoo at North Weald. Paul Bowen and Tim Prince had got a great programme together, we had cleared the runway and the peritrack, and cleaned one of the barrack blocks to accommodate the people flying in. Bob Basing was our engineering officer; Richard Holmes was in charge of reception; Paul's father, Pat, was on publicity; dear John Blake was on the microphone and Bill Newby-Grant and Chris Hammerbeck were engaged in – well, I can't quite remember, but something really useful.

*La Patrouille de France* team arrived on the rehearsal day with their Fouga Magisters, and flew a practice over our catchment area, which was an excellent advertisement. A little while afterwards, however, Richard strolled into my office. "We have a slight problem," he told me, "with the French. They totally reject the barrack block. Not up to their standard, apparently." (Incidentally, it may not be generally known that it was Richard who suggested 'Air Tattoo' when we were searching for a name.)

I found *La Patrouille*, all of whom were NCOs, sitting on their parachutes outside the offending building, looking rather glum, and a few cheery "Bonjours" didn't seem to do much good. The team manager was a Captain, who spoke a little English, and we contrived to reach an understanding. It amounted to this – no VIP accommodation, no display. Well, I was on a budget, as we always were, but what's money, after all? I took Richard aside. "Call the motel in Harlow," I said, "and lay on a coach."

When the Austrians came in, we wondered what their reaction to the barrack block might be. We need not have worried: "We are soldiers," said their leader, "and we sleep where we are put." We all liked the Austrians. But all credit to the French; they flew a great display, as did everybody else, the crowds rolled in, and everyone was happy – including, as I gathered, several chambermaids at the Harlow motel!

*Jack Currie*

## Second and last at North Weald

For Air Tattoo 72, the Spring Bank Holiday was again chosen as the date and North Weald the venue. Using the same management structure, the Air Tattoo team looked for solutions to the various problems encountered the previous year – traffic control, car parking and accommodation and transport for participants. A new problem encountered was brought about by the RAF's departure from North Weald, which had resulted in the deterioration of some of the paved surfaces.

Despite the worst Bank Holiday weather for many years, the airshow went ahead and once again included a number of items new to the UK and return

**AIR TATTOO'72**

Organised by the Royal Air Forces Association
Sponsored by
**W.D.& H.O.WILLS**

North Weald Airfield
Monday May 29th 1972

GATES OPEN - 10.00 a.m.
DISPLAYS COMMENCE - 11.00 a.m.
GATES CLOSE - 8.00 p.m.

SOUVENIR
PROGRAMME

Contrasting types on static display at North Weald in 1972 – US Navy Grumman C-1A Trader (top) and Britannia Airways Boeing 737. PRM

visits from overseas air arms such as Austria with Saab 105OEs, the Netherlands with a Breguet Atlantic and NF-5A, and Belgium with the *Diables Rouges* aerobatic team of Fouga Magisters. The American armed forces made a large contribution including a Sikorsky CH-54 Tarhe (Skycrane) from the US Army in Germany, and a Sikorsky HH-53C being refuelled by an HC-130 Hercules, both from the 67th Aerospace Rescue and Recovery Squadron, USAF at RAF Woodbridge.

As usual RAF participation was appreciable, including the *Red Pelicans* Jet Provost display team from the CFS, the *Vintage Pair* –

Below: Another airline participant at the 1972 Tattoo was Transmeridian's Canadair CL-44D G-AXAA. PRM

**On display at North Weald 1972 – Royal Netherlands Navy Breguet Atlantic (top) and Austrian Air Force Saab 105OE (above).** PRM

C-9A Nightingale being highlights of the USAF contribution. The US Navy sent a P-3C Orion, while the US Army provided a clutch of helicopters including the CH-54 Tarhe, a CH-47A Chinook, UH-1H Iroquois, AH-1G Cobra and OH-58A Kiowa. A whirling set-piece from the 7th Cavalry Regiment in the flying saw the skeletal Tarhe lifting a truck.

The Canadian Armed Forces put in a quartet of CF-104 Starfighters from No 439 Squadron which gave the first of many lively displays by various such teams using different names over the years. The French Navy supplied an SP-2H Neptune and an F-8E(FN) Crusader, the latter type giving a sparkling solo performance as it did 14 years later at IAT 87. Two Fleet Air Arm types soon to disappear from the scene, the Fairey Gannet AEW3 and DH110 Sea Vixen FAW2, were on show amongst the 30-strong static display. Winner of the *Embassy Solo Jet Aerobatic Display Trophy* was Flt Lt W. Tyndall flying a Jet Provost T5. At the end of the weekend a total of £13,000 was handed to RAFA, the proceeds from what aircrew, spectators, distinguished visitors and the organising team felt was a thoroughly enjoyable airshow.

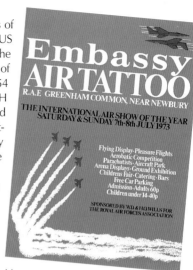

Meteor T7 and Vampire T11 – and the *Battle of Britain Memorial Flight*. Another RAF participant, Fg Off Rod Dean from No 79 Squadron, was awarded the new *Embassy Trophy* for the best solo jet performance in a Hunter. This trophy has continued to be awarded at each Air Tattoo by W.D. & H.O. Wills/Imperial Tobacco, although in recent years it has been known as the *Superkings Trophy*.

The outcome of Air Tattoo 72 was better than the organisers could have dared to hope, considering the poor weather which marred the day. The Tattoo team gained considerable experience, which was put to good use again that year with the first of two Goodwood Air Shows in August.

The major problem looming was to find a new location for future Tattoos. The M11 motorway was being constructed very close to the southwest end of the main runway and it was clear that the same layout would not be possible at North Weald for the duration of this work. Airfields seriously considered included Hurn, West Malling, Tangmere, Manston, Dunsfold and Odiham, but it was RAF Greenham Common, near Newbury, that was eventually selected thanks to the help and co-operation of the Base Commander and HQ Third Air Force, USAFE.

RAF Greenham Common was being maintained at this time by the 7551st Combat Support Group of the USAF as a NATO stand-by base. It was also providing a temporary home for Ugandan Asians who were waiting for resettlement in Britain. Amongst its assets was its huge size in terms of runway length and the hardstanding on which to park aircraft and cars, the vast majority of which was totally unused as there were no resident aircraft. One of its drawbacks was its proximity to the top secret Atomic Weapons Research Establishment at Aldermaston, which could not be overflown.

## The First Greenham Common

The Embassy Air Tattoo 1973, the first 'Greenham Common' as it became popularly known, took place on 7-8 July 1973. It continued the international bias established at North Weald with ten overseas air arms taking part. With more aircraft and an extensive ground display and trade exhibition, it was a logical step to run the event over two days. Highlights included heavyweight US support with a KC-97L from the 126th ARS, Wisconsin ANG, a C-141A Starlifter, and an aeromedical

**Wisconsin ANG Boeing KC-97L tanker at Greenham Common in 1973.** PRM

**The US Army CH-54A Tarhe demonstrating its lifting capabilities.** PRM

Greenham Common '73 – French Navy participation included this Vought F-8E (FN) Crusader (above) and Lockheed SP-2H Neptune (left). PRM

Below: US Army Grumman OV-1D Mohawk 17014. PRM

Below: Canadian Armed Forces CF-104 Starfighters on the operational apron. PRM

USAF C-121C Constellation of the 193rd Tactical Electronic Wing. PRM

## All Change

1974 was another turning point for the Air Tattoo team, with Jack Currie stepping down as the Tattoo Director. The airshow went ahead on the first weekend in July, the formula much the same as in 1973, with special attention being given to a wide variety of family attractions as well as the presentation of unusual aircraft for the enthusiasts. Again there was a venerable KC-97L, this time from the 160th ARG, Ohio ANG, and an even rarer C-121C Constellation of the 193rd Tactical Electronic Wing, Pennsylvania ANG but previously flown by Air America. The Austrian Air Force participated in the flying display, as did the Belgian Air Force with the *Swallows* SF.260 team, and the French Navy with a Crusader and Etendard IVP gave an in-flight refuelling demonstration. The late

Belgian Air Force Siai-Marchetti SF.260M ST-34 at the '74 Tattoo. PRM

Ormond Haydon-Baillie flew his Duxford-based T-33 Silver Star *Black Knight* and Sea Fury T20. From the RAF, Flt Lt Peter Chapman opened the display in a Lightning F3, a performance which earned him the year's *Embassy Trophy*. For many enthusiasts, the highlight was a flypast by a B-24J Liberator just after the *Red Arrows* had closed the Sunday show. This ex-Indian Air Force bomber was on a ferry flight from India to Colerne via Lyneham, destined for the RAF Museum, eventually going on to Cosford. Although short of fuel, as it had a leaking wing tank, the B-24 made a low-level flight along Greenham Common's 10,000ft runway.

**Embassy AIR TATTOO**
Sponsored by W. D. & H. O. Wills for the Royal Air Forces Association

R.A.F. Greenham Common

**NEWBURY 6th & 7th JULY 1974**

Featuring the world's top military aviators in competition for the Embassy Trophy.

**Souvenir Programme**

**15p**

Ormond Haydon-Baillie's all-black T-33 Silver Star G-OAHB *Black Knight* was on display at Greenham in 1974. PRM

**Winner of the 1974 *Embassy Trophy* was a Lightning F3.** PRM

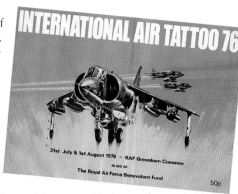

With a 50,000 crowd and a profit of more than £15,000, the last RAFA-controlled Air Tattoo was again very successful. However, the loss of Jack Currie as Director of the Tattoo, the withdrawal of overall sponsorship by W.D. & H.O. Wills and the international fuel crisis prevented there being an airshow at Greenham Common in 1975. Paul Bowen used this opportunity to put forward a proposal to the Royal Air Force Benevolent Fund, the upshot of which was that the RAF Benevolent Fund decided to support future Air Tattoos at Greenham Common using the Development Trust, which had been set up with the proceeds from a successful RAF Airshow at Farnborough in 1950.

## IAT and The RAF Benevolent Fund

Planning began for the first International Air Tattoo to be held at Greenham Common on 31 July and 1 August 1976. For the first time an aircraft type, the Hawker Hunter, was adopted as the focus of a 'meet'. As it was the 25th anniversary of the classic British jet fighter's first flight, the prototype, WB188, was brought in by road from St Athan and two dozen other examples were flown in to be lined up alongside it. The RAE's T7 XF321 was judged winner of the Hunter *Concours d'Elegance* competition.

Another special feature of IAT 76 was the appearance of no less than eight aerobatic teams from the 19 participating air arms, fully

justifying the addition of 'international' to the title. The Royal Navy's *Blue Herons* (four civilian-flown Hunter GA11s), the RAF *Gazelles* helicopter team and the *Red Arrows* (nine Gnat T1s), the Belgian Air Force *Diables Rouges* (six CM170R Magisters), the French Air Force *Patrouille de France* (nine more Magisters), the Italian Air Force *Frecce Tricolori* (nine Fiat G-91PANs), the Austrian Air Force *Karo As* (four Saab 105OEs) and the Canadian Air Force *Tiger Romeos* (four CF-104 Starfighters) all entertained splendidly. Equally spectacular was the civilian *Rothmans Team* flying Pitts Specials.

The US forces, appropriately enough in the American Bicentennial year, made their biggest showing yet – the F-111Es of the USAF's 79th TFS were resident at Greenham during runway resurfacing at Upper Heyford, with one of them bearing special Bicentennial colours. A rather older USAF type on static was another KC-97L, this time from the 181st ARS, Texas ANG. The US Navy contingent was most impressive, with an F-14A Tomcat, A-6E Intruder and A-7E Corsair (all in the display) plus S-3A Viking and E-2C Hawkeye being flown in off the USS *America*, while an EA-3B Skywarrior came from VQ-2 at Rota and was a highlight, just as a similar aircraft was at Fairford 15 years later.

**Participants at the 1976 Tattoo included US Navy aircraft from the USS *Dwight D. Eisenhower* – EA-6B Prowler, F-14A Tomcat and A-7E Corsair.** PRM

**On static display at Greenham in 1976 was this USAF F-111E in a special scheme to mark the US Bicentennial.**

**Top:** Part of the impressive line-up of Hawker Hunters at Greenham Common in 1976 to mark the type's 25th anniversary. GF

**Above:** The unusual pointed-nose Meteor NF11 from the RS&RE, one of many test aircraft that have appeared at IAT. GF

**Left:** Austrian Air Force Skyvan 5S-TB was also displayed in 1976. GF

Greenham 1976 – US Navy Grumman E-2C Hawkeye (top) and the four CF-104 Starfighters of the Canadian Armed Forces *Tiger Romeos* (above). GF

IAT 76 contributed in excess of £35,000 to the RAF Benevolent Fund from an attendance of over 120,000 people. The air show had been well regulated and safe, despite the large number of aerobatic teams and the inevitable competitive spirit amongst the crews. Winner of the solo jet *Embassy Trophy* was again the RAF, with Flt Lt David Webb's display in the Jet Provost judged to be the best performance. The late Peter Phillips, flying a Britten-Norman Defender, was recipient of the *Shell (UK) Oil Trophy* for the best overall flying performance, excluding jet aircraft and display teams.

## Tiger Meet and the Silver Jubilee

So on to 1977, which was to be the last of the annual Air Tattoos (for the time being, at least), but was also in itself very special, as it was the year of the Queen's Silver Jubilee. The NATO *Tiger Meet* was also to be held at Upper Heyford, home of the F-111Es of the 79th TFS – a USAF *Tiger Squadron*. It was switched to Greenham Common to fit in with the

Tattoo and 12 *Tiger* units took part, coming from Germany, Belgium, Canada, Italy, Norway and the USA. The RAF was represented in an honorary capacity by Puma-equipped No 230 Squadron, the Royal Australian Navy by No 816 Squadron with an S-2E Tracker from HMAS *Melbourne*, and the French Air Force with a Mirage F1 and a tiger-striped Super Mystere B2 from EC1/12. No 439 Squadron, Canadian Armed Forces was equally flamboyant in its application of the tiger scheme on the CF-104 Starfighters, the unit winning the *Mappin & Webb Silver Tiger Trophy* for the 'Spirit of the Meet'.

The Silver Jubilee International Air Tattoo on 25-26 June had representation from 21 air arms, including the Spanish and Portuguese Air Forces, the latter air arm creating a formation display team, the *Asas de Portugal* flying Cessna T-37Cs, specially for this event. The Royal Australian Navy's aircraft carrier HMAS *Melbourne* took part in the Silver Jubilee Review of the Fleet at

The Royal Navy *Blue Herons* Hunter team taking off at the 1977 show. GF

**A Royal Navy Buccaneer S2B of No 809 NAS took part in the 77 display.** PRM

Spithead and representative aircraft from her three squadrons flew in to Greenham. In addition to the *Tiger* squadron S-2 Tracker, there was a pair of A-4G Skyhawks from No 805 Squadron and a No 817 Squadron Sea King Mk50. Another carrier group taking part in the Silver Jubilee IAT came from the USS *John F. Kennedy*. The Royal Navy displayed a Buccaneer S2B from No 809 NAS, the last squadron to operate from HMS *Ark Royal*, nearing the end of its service with the RN.

On the final day of the 1977 air show, the RAF *Red Arrows* completed its 1,000th public display and ended the routine with a 'Jubilee Break'. Other teams taking part were the *Flying Jokers* comprising three F-5As from the Royal Norwegian Air Force, the *Vipers* helicopter team of two CH-136 Kiowas from the Canadian Armed Forces, and the Austrian Air Force *Karo As* making a return visit. In the 1977 flying display Oberleutnant Karl Zimmerman of the Federal German Army gave an outstanding aerobatic display in an MBB

**International visitors to Air Tattoo 77 included Royal Australian Navy A-4G Skyhawks (below) and the Cessna T-37Cs of the Portuguese *Asas de Portugal* aerobatic team, formed especially for the event (above right).** PRM

**Tiger-striped French Air Force Mystere B2 at the 1977 Tiger Meet.** PRM

BO105M helicopter and was awarded the *Nationwide Building Society International Display Sword*. The *Embassy Trophy* went yet again to the RAF, with Flt Lt Derek Fitzsimmons giving the best solo jet display in a Hawk T1. Derek Morter led the RN *Blue Herons* Hunter team to the well deserved award of the *Shell (UK) Oil Trophy*.

An important organisational development in 1977 was the introduction of the IAT Flying Control Committee. A team of eminent pilots established the flight safety rules and regulations for the flying

display, briefed the pilots each day and monitored their flying, both at rehearsal and during the displays. The committee had the power to stop a display if it was considered unsafe – a power that has been invoked on a number of occasions since. The constitution of this important team has contributed to the excellent safety record at IAT events and has since become a model for use at many major air events world-wide.

## Bassingbourn Interlude

While there was no IAT the following year, the organising team was kept very busy through not only the planning for 1979's Tattoo, but also with the staging of another major event, the Anglo-American Air Festival at Bassingbourn on 27-28 May 1978. This was the climax of a week-long series of events mounted for veterans of the 91st Bomb Group, the occupants of the Cambridgeshire airfield between 1942-45. Invited by the Army and the East Anglian Aviation Society to present a two-day international air display in commemoration of the 91st, IAT re-opened the airfield (home of the Depot, The Queen's Division) 40 years after it was first opened by the RAF in 1938.

Fittingly, B-17G Flying Fortress *Sally B*, then owned by the late Don Bullock's Euroworld Ltd, was present, remembering the B-17s of the 91st BG. It was joined by the same company's A-26C Invader, a 'surprise item' on the programme and making one of its first appearances.

**US Navy F-14A Tomcat 159601 came from the USS *John F. Kennedy*.** PRM

**Three Harvards from the A&AEE at Boscombe Down at Bassingbourn.** PRM

An international meet of North American T-6s/Harvards celebrated the famous trainer's 40th anniversary, with aircraft from the UK, the Netherlands, Sweden, France and Germany all present. The four-hour flying display included excellent RAF participation, including the *Red Arrows* and a spectacular Battle Demonstration from RAF Wessex and Buccaneers, supported by the home-based Queen's Division. The Canadian Armed Forces sent its *Tiger Romeos* team of CF-104 Starfighters, and the USAF provided a number of items in what was a very special climax to a memorable week of events for the USAAF veterans.

**Air Tattoo 79 –** *Royal Jordanian Falcons* **Pitts S-2 Special JY-RJG.** PRM

## Bigger and better

The International Air Tattoos in 1979, 1981 and 1983 became bigger and better, following the pattern established in having a number of special aeronautical features and a wide range of family entertainment. At IAT 79 on 23-24 June, the 25th anniversary of the C-130 Hercules was marked with a line-up of 25 of the type headed by the first C-130A delivered to the USAF in 1956, 55-0023 *City of Ardmore* from the 185th TAS, Oklahoma ANG. A Hercules Industries Team, led by the Lockheed-Georgia company, sponsored an operator's symposium and looked after the social needs of the C-130 crews from all over the world. Indeed, Hercules arrived from far and wide to take part – the

**The 25th anniversary of the Hercules was marked in 1979 with an impressive international line-up of C-130s from across the world.** Martin Horseman

*Concours d'Elegance* was won by a C-130E of No 40 Squadron, Royal New Zealand Air Force, while air arms from Saudi Arabia, Argentinia and Israel were also represented. Among the unusual derivatives in the line were the RAF Meteorological Research Flight's Hercules W2 XV208, and from the USAF a ski-equipped C-130D of the 139th TAS, New York ANG.

Other anniversaries marked in 1979 were the 60th anniversary of the first non-stop trans-Atlantic crossing by Alcock and Brown in a Vickers Vimy in 1919 and the 30th anniversary of NATO. An RAF Phantom FGR2 was specially painted to mark both of these anniversaries and flown non-stop across the Atlantic, arriving at Greenham Common in 5hr 40min from Goose Bay. The pilot for the flight was Sqn Ldr Tony Alcock, a nephew of Capt John Alcock who made the first historic crossing.

The appearance of two Pitts S-2 Specials in the colours of the Jordanian state airline Alia, flying as the *Royal Jordanian Falcons* aerobatic team heralded the start of a long association between IAT and Jordan, which was to culminate in HM King Hussein becoming Patron of IAT. 1979 saw the end of the RAF's domination of the *Embassy Solo Jet Aerobatic Trophy*, with the Austrian AF Saab 105OE flown by Oberleutnant Wolf taking the award. The *Nationwide Display Sword* went to Maj *Boy* Soons of No 334 Squadron, Royal Netherlands AF who gave a breathtaking aerobatic display in the F-27-300M Troopship.

With the crowd total reaching 160,000 and a profit of £125,000, IAT 79 was a great success. Since the previous event at Greenham, Friends of the International Air Tattoo (FIAT) had been established, and IAT 79 was the first to feature a crowd-line enclosure and facilities for FIAT members. A lasting memory for many of Sunday's visitors will be the torrential storm in the morning which turned the static aircraft park into a lake. The C-5A Galaxy provided shelter for what has been estimated at over 1,000 people.

**Sir Douglas Bader (right) greets Sqn Ldr Alcock and Flt Lt Browne after their arrival at Air Tattoo 79 in the specially painted RAF Phantom FGR2.** PRM

**This Royal Norwegian Air Force F-5B appeared at Greenham in 1980.** BSS

## Newbury Air Festival

The following year, the volunteer team was back in action at Greenham Common for the Newbury Air Festival on 31 May and 1 June 1980, an event which had experienced possibly the most difficult gestation period of any arranged by IAT. This was a display of more aerial contrasts than an Air Tattoo, and had originally been planned at the request of Bristol City Council to mark the 50th anniversary of the opening of the municipal airport at Whitchurch on 31 May 1930, and was originally to have taken place at Bristol (Lulsgate) Airport. However, following original planning, it became clear that such a busy commercial airport could not be used for a major airshow, and the Bristol International Air Festival was moved to the BAe airfield at Filton. There, it would mark 70 years of Bristol aircraft 'from Boxkite to Concorde' and 60 years of Bristol aero engines.

Sadly, BAe withdrew permission to use Filton just ten weeks before the event, whereupon another alternative had to be found. Greenham Common was the only remaining choice, and, thanks to support from all concerned at short notice, the Air Festival was finally re-located for the last time. Proceedings were opened by displays of hot-air balloons, hang-gliders and man-powered aircraft – quite different items from those at an IAT. The rest of the programme contained plenty of foreign military metal including the Canadian Forces five-ship of CF-104s, the Austrian Air Force *Karo As*, Royal Norwegian Air Force F-5As and a French Air Force Mirage F1, alongside the regular RN and RAF items. The static park, though smaller than that at an IAT, was certainly diverse – indeed, bearing in mind the changes of venue, the whole staging of the Air Festival was a great achievement by the volunteer team.

**The Royal Navy Historic Flight's Firefly taxies past the operational apron.** GF

Making its debut at Greenham Common in 1980 – a Canadian Armed Forces CC-132 based at Lahr, West Germany. BSS

## SeaSearch

The main theme for IAT 81 on 27-28 June was maritime operations, under the title SeaSearch 81. Participants, both helicopters and fixed-wing aircraft, arrived early in the week and took part in flying and ground competitions. Victory in the fixed-wing competition went, surprisingly, to the civilian BAe Coastguarder. Part of the helicopter competition took place at Bowood House, Wiltshire, where a slalom course was set out on the lawns in front of the fine mansion. This was followed by a major symposium which dealt specifically with search and rescue.

A second major theme in 1981 was the 40th anniversary of the first flight of a British turbojet-powered aircraft. There was an impressive line-up of different types representing 40 years of British jet power in the static display, and an hour devoted to these aircraft in the flying programme. At the opposite ends of the time and speed scales, IAT 81 presented a World War I dog-fight involving replica aircraft specially constructed for Leisure Sport at Thorpe Park, and in complete contrast the new Tornado F2 air defence variant from BAe Warton. The rather less successful Nimrod AEW3 was another interesting item, with an RAF Shackleton AEW2 also appearing in the display.

In a most varied programme, there were again plenty of formation teams, among them two teams with new equipment since their previous IAT outings – the *Red Arrows* flying Hawks and *La Patrouille de France* now with Alpha Jets. As part of a strong Canadian Forces contingent, a five-ship of CF-104s, this time named the *Starfighters*, made its last Tattoo appearance. The Royal Netherlands Air Force swept the board in the flying display awards with the *Grasshoppers* and F-27 displays, while No 11 Squadron, Royal Jordanian Air Force provided F-5E Tiger IIs, and 332 Skv of the Royal Norwegian Air Force flew an F-16A – the first Fighting Falcon display at IAT.

For the first time over 200,000 people attended an IAT in 1981. It

SEA SEARCH 81
**International Air Tattoo 81**
Newbury 27, 28 June
In aid of the Royal Air Force Benevolent Fund and in association with Nationwide Building Society
IAT

Above: SeaSearch 81 participation from Spain was provided by this SAR F-27M. GF

Below: All-white Canadian Armed Forces CC-115 Buffalo at the 1981 Tattoo. GF

The four Saab 105s of the Austrian Air Force *Karo As* aerobatic team waiting for take-off at Air Tattoo 81. GF

**Above:** On static display at Greenham in 1981, A&AEE Canberra WV787 from Boscombe Down was modified for icing trials. GF

Colourful tiger-striped Canadian Armed Forces CF-104 (above) and the Alpha Jets of the *Patrouille de France* aerobatic team (inset). PRM

Eye-catching F-5A K-3026 of the Royal Netherlands Air Force. GF

Army Air Corps Gazelles at the Army Air 82 show at Middle Wallop. GF

Spencer Flack's privately-owned Sea Fury FB.11 G-FURY at Greenham. GF

## Salute to Sir Douglas Bader

In the interim period before IAT 83, the organising team faced various worries at Greenham Common. The USAF's build-up in preparation for the arrival of its cruise missile deployment caused anxiety in some quarters as to whether or not the event could be staged at all, and the resulting presence of the anti-missile campaigners' 'peace camp' outside the base's main gate threatened problems, but for the most part these failed to materialise and the 1983 show on 23-24 July was the biggest and best yet, with nearly 400 aircraft involved. A salute to the late Sir Douglas Bader, IAT's President for seven years, was staged as one of the principal themes, with a gathering of two Hurricanes and seven Spitfires paying tribute. The other theme was the STAR (Strike, Attack and Reconnaissance) 83 meet,

was again a bigger and better air show with a large sum donated to the RAF Benevolent Fund. Sadly though, 1981 was the last IAT to be attended by its President, Sir Douglas Bader. The following year, the organising team was involved in the staging of Army Air 82 at the Army Air Corps Centre, Middle Wallop – the first of four biennial Army Air and then International Air Shows at the Hampshire grass airfield arranged jointly by the AAC and IAT.

Aviation's Tribute to Sir Douglas Bader
International Air Tattoo JULY 23-24
RAF GREENHAM COMMON NEWBURY, BERKS

Hurricanes and Spitfires gathered at Greenham in 1983 as a tribute to Sir Douglas Bader. PRM

International
Air Tattoo 83

RAF GREENHAM COMMON
Newbury, Berks
23/24 July

Above: Phantom FG1 XT863 of No 111 Sqn was the F-4 *Concours d'Elegance* winner at the 1983 show. APM

Left: The Aermacchi MB.339s of the Italian Air Force *Frecce Tricolori* aerobatic team. PRM

Aerial view of the 1983 Air Tattoo, with much attention being given to the SR-71 Blackbird and TR-1 at the end of the STAR 83 line-up. GF

**A&AEE Phantom FG1 XT597 received a special colour scheme for the 1983 Tattoo, designed by renowned aviation artist Wilf Hardy (right).** APM

combined with celebrations for the 25th anniversary of the F-4 Phantom.

The STAR line-up included the USAF's SR-71A and TR-1A on show together for the first time at a Tattoo, these certainly attracting much attention. USN carrier aircraft from the USS *Dwight D. Eisenhower* and IAT's last big gathering of F-104s (from Belgium, Canada, Denmark and West Germany) were also notable. The line of 27 F-4 Phantoms from the RAF, USAF and Federal German Air Force was also impressive, among them the A&AEE's Phantom FG1 XT597 bearing a special anniversary colour scheme (in large-scale transfer form) designed by Wilf Hardy and painstakingly applied following arrival at Greenham.

In the air over the weekend, there were seven national display teams, among them the *Frecce Tricolori* making its first UK visit flying ten new Aermacchi MB.339A/PANs. The Westl German Navy *Vikings* with their F-104Gs from MFG-2, Royal Jordanian Air Force Mirage F1EJ of No 1 Squadron, a colourful Royal Netherlands Air Force NF-5A and F-16A and in particular the Royal Norwegian Air Force F-16A (which many felt should have been among the flying prizewinners) all gave exciting displays, but the RAF Lightning F3 flown by Flt Lt Thompson from the LTF won the *Superkings Trophy*. Capt Zimmerman of the

Federal German Army was even more successful than he had been at IAT 77, being awarded the *International Display Sword* and the *Sir Douglas Bader Trophy* for his aerobatic routine in a BO105M. A regular item at several Air Tattoos, the Goodyear airship *Europa*, made its final appearance.

This was once again a memorable and very successful Tattoo, but it had not been without its problems. The anti-cruise missile campaigners had, for the most part, remained peaceful although the SR-71 and a KC-135 were daubed with paint by demonstrators who entered the airfield on the Sunday night. There were other difficulties as well. Lt-Cdr Witte and his crew flying Atlantic 61+13 of the Federal German Navy's MFG-3 had a fraught time – all

**A&AEE Britannia XX397 made the type's last visit to IAT in 1983.** GF

**Captured during the Falklands War, Pucara ZD485 flew in to IAT 83.** GF

**The Goodyear airship *Europa* made its final IAT appearance in 1983.** APM

four mainwheel tyres burst on landing following his practice display on the Thursday, and in order not to block the runway Lt-Cdr Witte taxied clear. The aircraft thus required new wheels, which were flown in aboard another Atlantic and fitted in time for Saturday's show. However, during its routine, a bird-strike on 'unlucky 61+13' caused an engine shutdown. At the Sunday night prizegiving, Lt-Cdr Witte and his crew were presented with the trophy for *Best Hard Luck Story* and

**Right: Specially painted F-16A of No 322 Sqn, Royal Netherlands Air Force waits for take-off, with RAE Viscount XT661 on finals.** PRM

**Below: West German Navy Atlantic 'unlucky' 61+13.** GF

**Royal Jordanian Air Force Mirage F1 landing at Greenham 83.** GF

**Flypast by the USAF SR-71A Blackbird on arrival at IAT 83.** GF

the British Airways stewardesses' award for the *Most Outstanding Landing*.

There were problems too for the *Asas de Portugal*, when two of its T-37s collided at the end of their landing run on arrival due to braking difficulties. A pair of replacement aircraft were flown in and the team was able to fly over the weekend. Another difficult arrival was that of the B-52G from Dyess AFB, an electrical fault resulting in the absence of confirmation that its wheels were locked down. After several low passes for visual checks of its undercarriage, the Stratofortress – callsign *Bowen 13* – thankfully made a safe landing.

**USAF B-52G from Dyess AFB flies low over Greenham for visual checks of its undercarriage before landing.** GF

**USAF participation in 1983 included a camouflaged EC-130 Hercules.** GF

**Characteristic display by the Royal Netherlands Air Force F-27 Troopship.** GF

## A new home

The seven Tattoos at Greenham Common had firmly established the event as the foremost of its type in the world, having presented some fascinating spectacles. However, the build-up of the USAF's cruise missile facilities made it impractical for IAT to continue operation at the Berkshire base. In spite of numerous requests from Greenham's Base Commander for the show to remain, the RAF Benevolent Fund had to find a new venue, with several candidates being narrowed down to RAF Fairford in Gloucestershire and RAE Bedford/Thurleigh. The former, in the same catchment area as Greenham and another USAF base, was of course the final choice.

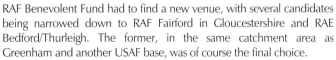

The team, under Tim Prince and Paul Bowen, overcame major organisational hurdles in moving the show to an airfield which was then an important operational base, housing the KC-135s on temporary duty (TDY) with the USAF's 11th Strategic Group, and other problems. IAT 85 on 13-14 July kicked off the third (Fairford-based) period in IAT's history in fine style, with over 200,000 people in attendance.

Appropriately, bearing in mind the new venue's operational role, SkyTanker was the year's main theme, with the largest assembly of air-to-air refuellers ever seen dominating the static park. Débuts from a newly-delivered RAF VC10 K3, French Transall C-160NG tanker, Federal German Navy Tornado 'buddy-tanker', plus USAF KC-135R and grey-painted KC-10A were welcomed by enthusiasts, but all were beaten in the *Concours d'Elegance* by the KC-135E 56-3611 of the 145th ARS, Ohio ANG. In the air, two KC-135s from the 11th SG opened the show, and an EC-135H from the 10th ACCS at Mildenhall flying through with three 20th TFW F-111Es – one of them actually hooked-up – closed it. In between, the RAF impressed with a flypast from a Hercules C1K, Victor K2, VC10 K2 and the first Tristar K1 conversion, flown for the first time only a few days before from Marshall of Cambridge. The French Navy contributed a 'buddy-buddy' refuelling demo with an Etendard IVP leading a Super Etendard.

The Skytanker 85 line-up (top) was dominated by USAF KC-135s and featured the first appearance by a grey-painted USAF KC-10A (above). Winner of the *Concours d'Elegance* was a KC-135E from the Ohio ANG (below). PRM

**Below: RAF participants in Skytanker 85 – VC10 K3 and Victor K2.** JD

**Above: Eight of the DC-3s that attended the 50th anniversary celebrations.** PRM

The second theme was the 50th anniversary of the Douglas DC-3/C-47, and ten were brought together at Fairford. Two of them, Col Tom Thomas' DC-3 and the Confederate Air Force's R4D-8S, were flown across from the USA just to appear. RAE Farnborough's Dakota C3 ZA947 (now with the *BBMF*) carried special 50th anniversary colours designed by Wilf Hardy, while just as colourful was the Italian Air Force EC-47A of 14 Stormo which was adjudged to be runner up in the Page Engineering Dakota *Concours d'Elegance*. The winner was an aircraft now very familiar to airshow-goers, the Dutch Dakota Association's DC-3 PH-DDA.

For various reasons, there were few overseas aerobatic teams present, and RAF participation was limited due to fuel shortages. However, the *Red Arrows* were of course present, formating with British Airways Concorde G-BOAG, while the *BBMF* flew its Spitfire PRXIX PM631 with a No 229 OCU Tornado F2. The appearances of the Federal German Navy *Vikings* duo of F-104Gs and four more in close formation from the Federal German Air Force's LVsuRgt-1 (test unit) were significant – Starfighters have never been seen again in an IAT flying display. The new *Superkings Solo Jet Aerobatic Trophy* went to Major Eric Nedergaard of the 36th TFW, USAFE, flying the F-15C Eagle, with Capt Charly Zimmerman for the third time winning the *Nationwide International Display Sword* for his performance in the German BO105. The other flying prizewinner was Sqn Ldr Jolyon Maclean, pilot of the RAF SKTU's Sea King HAR3, who took home the *Sir Douglas Bader Trophy*.

**Colourful participants at the DC-3/C-47 celebrations were an Italian Air Force EC-47A and the RAE's Dakota C3 ZA947, the latter carrying special markings for the occasion.** PRM

## Bournemouth and WAC 86

Following on from IAT 85, the organising team turned its attentions to another venue, Bournemouth (Hurn) International Airport for its second TVS Air Show South, sponsored by the then regional television company. The first IAT-organised show at the Dorset airfield (one of those on the original shortlist for the Tattoo's home before the choice of Greenham Common), in August 1984, had been a success, following on from the popularity of the earlier Bournemouth Air Pageants. The 1986 display was bigger and better, but the Saturday flying programme was all but wiped out by atrocious weather conditions. Notable items on the Sunday included the last display at an IAT show by the Federal German Navy *Vikings*, the 2000th public performance by the *Red*

**The ex-Argentinian Air Force Bell UH-1H G-HUEY at Bournemouth.** APM

**The Federal German Navy** *Vikings* **duo flying two F-104G Starfighters at the TVS International Air Show 86.** JD

**The three Sukhoi Su-26Ms of the Soviet national team at WAC 86.** PRM

*Arrows* and the début of IAT's own ex-Argentinian Air Force Bell UH-1H G-HUEY, restored by Rob Tierney. MoD(PE), the French Navy, Spanish Air Force and USAF all made good contributions, as did the home-based operators with FR Aviation's F-100F Super Sabre making a rare outing.

That same year, only a few miles away from its home, IAT arranged the 13th World Aerobatic Championships at South Cerney – 'just up the road' from Fairford – including the World Festival of Aerobatics Airshow on 16 August. Undoubted stars of the display were three Sukhoi Su-26Ms of the Soviet national team, following their victory in the Championships, which performed an exhilarating celebration routine. Other competition machines in the programme included new French CAP230s, Czechoslovak and Hungarian Zlin 50s and various aircraft from the US team. The *Red Arrows* and other RAF items, USAF A-10 and F-16, the Czech support Antonov An-2 and a BA Concorde made this a diverse and entertaining airshow following an intriguing World Championship.

## Fairford grows

Back at Fairford, with the inaugural event there completed, the organising team received much support from the enthusiastic based USAF personnel in planning IAT 87, which would have two operational themes – SkyLift, a gathering of transport aircraft, and SkyShield – a celebration of 75 years of UK air defence. Aircraft from 19 nations were on display on 18-19 July, making this the most international Air Tattoo since the first in 1971, but proceedings were dampened by the appalling summer weather, especially on the Sunday when a three-hour downpour halted the flying display and turned Fairford into a quagmire.

However, this was still a superb event. The SkyLift *Wings of Peace* meet saw a mile-long line of airlifters put together in the static park, including a 16-strong USAF contingent, this of course including some of the large C-130 Hercules selection which further featured examples from such distant countries as Jordan and Chile. It was the USAF who scooped the SkyLift *Concours d'Elegance*, with the crew of KC-135E 55-3146 from the 160th ARG/145th ARS, Ohio ANG, taking away with them the *Page Aerospace Trophy*.

Other interesting static items included several rare USAF types. A-7D and A-7K Corsair IIs from the Pennsylvania and New Mexico ANGs were present during UK deployments, with the 509th BW flying in two FB-111As just to appear at Fairford. An early AC-130A, 55-0011 from the 711th SOS, AFRes, and two EC-130 variants – an EC-130E of the 193rd SOS, Pennsylvania ANG and an EC-130H of the 43rd ECS were also notable.

National display teams were much greater in number this time, with nine in total including several returnees, among them the *Frecce Tricolori* who particularly delighted the audience. Newcomers were the Spanish Air Force *Patrulla Aguila* with its C-101 Aviojets, *Los Halcones* of the Chilean Air Force flying Pitts S-2s and the two CAP10s of the Royal Moroccan Air Force *Marche Verte*. The French Air Force provided the exceptional *Phoenix* aeromedical parachute team, jumping for the first time in the UK. The familiar *Grasshoppers* of the Royal Netherlands Air Force won two of the display prizes, namely the *International Display Sword* and *Sir Douglas Bader Trophy*. The third, the *Superkings Trophy*, went to Flt Lt Paul Brown of the RAF's No 229 OCU, flying the Tornado F3, in spite of Sunday's dreadful weather. Another outstanding fast jet performance came from the F-8E(FN) Crusader of 12F, French Navy. The Royal Jordanian Air Force's solo Mirage F1EJ, and the *Royal Jordanian Falcons* Pitts trio, were enthusiastically watched on the Sunday by HM King Hussein who had earlier made his own flypast on arrival in the Royal Flight TriStar.

**Visitors to IAT '87 – French Navy F-8E(FN) Crusader (below) and Swedish Air Force C-130E/Tp-8 (bottom).** PRM

**Above: Flying display aircraft on the operational apron at IAT 87.** PRM

**Above & left: Views of the extensive Skylift line-up at IAT 87.** PRM

SkyLifters in the flying were led by the massed formation of 15 Lyneham-based Hercules C1/C3s. In fact, a third of the total LTW fleet participated over the weekend. None of these displays was as exuberant, though, as that of the Swedish Air Force's C-130E/Tp84 which was flung around with gusto. Apart from the Tornado F3, the SkyShield theme was represented in the air by UK air defenders past and present, including a Hurricane and three Spitfires from the *BBMF*, and what was the last IAT display by an RAF Lightning, this time an F3 version from No 5 Squadron.

**Below: Massed formation flypast by 15 RAF Hercules C1/C3s.** GF

**Top:** Belgian Air Force Mirage V specially painted to mark the 70th anniversary of No 1 Sqn. GF

**Above:** Aerobatic demonstration by the Pitts Specials of the Chilean Air Force's *Los Halcones* team. PRM

**Left:** CASA 101 Aviojets of the Spanish Air Force *Patrulla Aguilla*. PRM

**Above: A highlight of the TVS show was the aerobatic display by *La Patrouille Martini*, flying Pilatus PC-7s.** APM

**Below: The Yugo Stearman taking-off to perform a wing-walking routine at the 1988 Bournemouth show.** GF

A third TVS Air Show at Bournemouth on 4-5 June 1988 was IAT's next event, and again was very successful. The static display was excellent, featuring large-scale RAF support and plenty from the US forces. The star USAF static item was undoubtedly an A-7D Corsair II of the 138th TFG, Oklahoma ANG, on deployment to the UK, which was a last-minute addition arriving on the Saturday evening. The 25th anniversary of the BAC 1-11 was marked by three aircraft (from the RAE, Ryanair and the UAE) in the static on the first day. Among the highlights of the flying was *La Patrouille Martini* with its three Pilatus PC-7s spitting flame from their smoke generators. This was IAT's last event at Bournemouth, but the three TVS Air Shows had provided much entertainment and of course good contributions for the RAF Benevolent Fund.

## Hottest show

Without doubt, for all present, the weather was an abiding memory of 1987's event. Two years later, it was again a major feature of proceedings, but at IAT 89 on 22-23 July record-breaking temperatures (reaching 34°C/94°F) and unbeaten hours of scorching sunshine saw to it that RAF Fairford welcomed the highest-ever Tattoo attendance. This show, marking 40 years since the formation of NATO and, as in 1981 (and of course this year), taking SeaSearch as its operational theme, was the focus of additional attention from worldwide following the terrible tragedy at Ramstein the previous year. After the debates and discussion

**The USAF's 'SAC Attack' was one of the highlights at IAT 89, featuring a B-1B Lancer (top), B-52G Stratofortress (above) and FB-111A (inset).** GF

surrounding the future of air displays that followed the disaster in Germany, it was most pleasing that this was yet another incident-free IAT.

Adding to the searing heat was plenty of noise, especially from the USAF's Strategic Air Command whose contribution was, for most spectators, the undoubted highlight. What turned out to be the last

display on these shores by an SR-71A from Mildenhall's 9th SRW/Det 4 stole the show on the Sunday, while on both days the *SAC Attack* sequence with a stream take-off by one of the home-based 11th SG's KC-135Rs, FB-111A of the 380th BW, a 319th BW B-1B, and a B-52G from the 2nd BW followed by individual flybys from each proved most

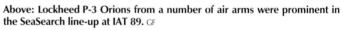

Above: Lockheed P-3 Orions from a number of air arms were prominent in the SeaSearch line-up at IAT 89. GF

Left: Welcome first-time visitor to IAT was a Portuguese Air Force SA330C Puma, also taking part in the SeaSearch Meet. GF

Below: SAR-configured Casa C.212 Aviocar of the Spanish Air Force. PRM

impressive. Of the three bombers, only the Stratofortress had ever been seen in an IAT flying display before.

Twenty-nine aircraft from 18 air arms of ten different countries, plus civilian types, formed the International SeaSearch Meet static park. Among the prizewinners were the colourful US Coast Guard HC-130H from Borinquen and the HH-65A Dauphin that came in its hold, but the Page Aerospace *Concours d'Elegance* winner was the Royal Australian Air Force C-130E from No 37 Squadron, whose crew also took home the Graviner *Spirit of the Meet* trophy and the *Rolls-Royce Trophy* as ground competition winners. They were just beaten to the *Holiday Inn Trophy* for the crew that travelled the greatest distance to attend by that of the Royal New Zealand Air Force's P-3K Orion, that was also the *Concours d'Elegance* runner-up. Other notable SeaSearchers included the Portuguese Air Force SA330C Puma from Esq 751, an SAR-configured C-212 Aviocar of the Spanish Air Force and four civilian contributions – the FR Aviation-operated Dornier 228 of MAFF, the Pollution Control

Cessna 402 and DC-3 flown by the Atlantic Group, and another C-212 from the Swedish Coast Guard. In the air, a three-ship RAF Nimrod MR2 formation from the Kinloss MR Wing impressed, as did the Bristow Helicopters S-61N operated on behalf of HM Coastguard and the *Windmills*, the Royal Netherlands Navy's SH-14 Lynx duo.

Not all the static attention was focused on maritime aircraft however, particularly with the USAF's input. Alongside the SR-71 there was another FB-111, B-52 and B-1B plus an RC-135 and six KC-135s. Two A-7Ds from the 112th TFG, Pennsylvania ANG were flown across just to appear in the IAT static park, while the pair of 23rd TFW A-10As present were on detachment in Germany from their base at England AFB. The rather scruffy Greek Air Force A-7H and TA-7H from 345 Mira contrasted with the immaculate NF-5s and F-16s of the Royal Netherlands Air Force, with other Fighting Falcons coming from the USAF, Denmark and Norway. Closer to home, MoD(PE) sent 19 aircraft for the static including RAE Llanbedr's Meteor D16 WH453 making a very rare outing.

1989's *Superkings Trophy* winner was Flt Lt Simon Meade from No 2 TWU/151 Squadron at Chivenor, flying a Hawk T1A through what was adjudged the best solo jet sequence.

It was *Los Halcones* of the Chilean Air Force with their four Pitts S-2As that scooped the *International Display Sword* for the best routine by an overseas participant, while the stunning aerobatic antics of Italian Air Force Reparto Sperimentale Volo test pilot, Lt-Col Giovanni Ammoniaci, in his Aeritalia G222 saw

**International Air Tattoo 89**

**RAF FAIRFORD 22-23 JULY**
CIRENCESTER, GLOS
SUPPORTED BY
**Canon** South West

**US Coast Guard HC-130H landing at IAT 89.** PRM

**The aircraft that travelled the greatest distance to attend IAT 89 was the Royal New Zealand Air Force P-3K Orion.** PRM

him take away the Shell (UK) Oil *Sir Douglas Bader Trophy* for the best overall display sequence.

The eight and a half hours of flying featured six national military and two civilian aerobatic teams, foremost among them the *Red Arrows* marking its 25th anniversary. The pilot of the Canberra PR9 from No 1 PRU suffered a rather less celebratory weekend. Following a contretemps with the Flying Control Committee after his Saturday slot,

**On static display at IAT 89 – Greek Air Force A-7H Corsair (right) and RAF Victor K2 (below), making a low pass on arrival at Fairford.** PRM/GF

**Aerial view of part of the static display at Fairford in 1989, including a variety of types flown by the ETPS and A&AEE at Boscombe Down.** PRM

RAE Llanbedr-based Meteor D16 WH453 was a welcome highlight in 1989. GF

he took no further part in the flying display. IAT Patron, King Hussein, once again arrived at the controls of the Jordanian Royal Flight TriStar before then watching the *Royal Jordanian Falcons* Pitts Specials and the RJAF's solo Mirage F1 flown in immaculate fashion. Other unusual attendees such as the manufacturer's demonstrator ENAER T-35 Pillan, Hungarian Air Services' crop-spraying Antonov An-2 and *les Fanatiques d'Aviation*'s visiting Hurel-Dubois HD34 made this a most varied weekend of aerial action. Though the temperature did cause its own problems of heat exhaustion and other related difficulties, the record attendance of over 250,000, and the resulting highest-ever donation to the RAF Benevolent Fund, made this possibly one of the most successful IATs to date.

Notable visitors in 1989 were the Jordanian Royal Flight TriStar (above) flown in by King Hussein, and the distinctive Hurel-Dubois HD34 (inset). APM

## Battle of Britain Anniversary

After IAT 89, the organising team turned its attention to the preparation of events for the following summer, as 1990 would see the 50th anniversary of the Battle of Britain. The Benevolent Fund's *Reach for the Sky* appeal aimed to raise £20 million in recognition of this, and appropriately and uniquely, IAT was granted use of the MoD(PE) airfield at A&AEE Boscombe Down in Wiltshire, an RAF Fighter Command base during the Battle itself, for its 'alternate year' event arranged in association with TVS. On 16 August 1940, flying a Hurricane from Boscombe Down, Flt Lt James Nicolson won Fighter Command's only Victoria Cross of WW2, making this an even more poignant occasion.

On 9-10 June 1990, 19 nations contributed military aircraft to the Battle of Britain Air Show, with 27 air arms being represented. However, it was the gathering of 12 Spitfires and two Hurricanes for the *Battle of Britain Aerial Pageant*, the anniversary set-piece, that of course was the highlight. On the Saturday, strong winds prevented Fighter Command from getting airborne to beat off the two attacking Messerschmitt Bf109J/HA1112 Buchons and Bf108, but the second day saw better conditions and the full sequence could be

presented, concluding with a *missing man* flypast from the Spitfires and Hurricanes as the final salute to *the Few*. Following in a more modern vein, the closing item was a noisy scramble of four Phantom FGR2s from No 56 Squadron, depicting some of 1990's air defenders.

Eight hours of flying appropriately took in items from several of the WW2 Allied air forces, including the *SAC Attack* take-off and display from the USAF B-52G and B-1B. The Royal Australian Air Force's F-111C 'torching' routine, provided by No 1 Squadron, was seen in the UK for the first time since the RAF Finningley Royal Review in 1977, while other particularly notable showings were made by four CF-188 Hornets from the Canadian Armed Forces, French Air Force Mirage 2000 from

**Aerial views of aircraft on display in 1990 – Spitfires and Hurricanes (right) and more modern military hardware (below), with several specially marked RAF Tornados in the foreground.** PRM

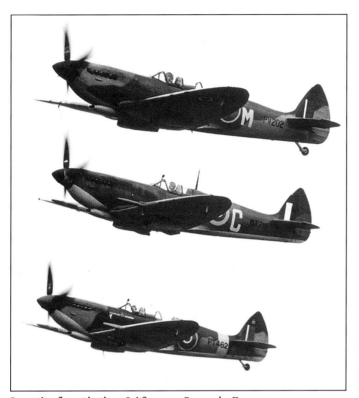

**Formation flypast by three Spitfires over Boscombe Down.** JD

time since 1981 with its Hunter F58s.

In the static, it was not surprising but very welcome to see over 30 test and trials aircraft lined up, from veterans such as the two based A&AEE Harvards, Comet 4C and the damaged Sea Fury T20S, ETPS Hunters, RAE Canberras and the Llanbedr Meteor to the Tornado F2 and the Harrier GR5A being evaluated by the A&AEE. Another classic jet on show was the Vampire T55 donated by the Swiss Air Force to the RAF Benevolent Fund, which is now operated by the Royal Jordanian Air Force Historic Flight.

Other foreigners such as another Australian F-111C, Hellenic Air Force Mirage 2000 of 332 Mira and two Jordanian Mirage F1s and a large Portuguese contingent comprising a 502 Esq C-212ECM, A-7Ps from 302 Esq and T-38A Talons of 102 Esq made this a most varied static park, but again the US forces dominated. Aside from the SAC visitors, Stateside-based machinery on show from the USAF included four 33rd FW F-15C/Ds from Eglin AFB, a rarely-seen 375th AAW T-39A Sabreliner and 323rd FTW T-43A, while the Coast Guard (with HC-130, HH-65 and an HU-25A Guardian) and Marine Corps also contributed, as did the US Navy. Four different types – an A-6E, S-3B, F-14A+ and F/A-18A – were flown in off the USS *Dwight D. Eisenhower*, the first such appearance by USN carrier-borne types at a UK event for some years.

EC2/2 (the type's first IAT appearance), a colourful Royal Netherlands Air Force F-16A and, for the first time ever, the Czechoslovaks with a specially-marked L-39 Albatros from Aero Vodochody. Another interesting trainer was the Royal Jordanian Air Force C-101 Aviojet. The *Red Arrows* were joined on the display team bill by *La Patrouille de France*, *Patrulla Aguila*, and the *Patrouille Suisse* returning for the first

**Royal Netherlands Air Force F-16A Fighting Falcon using its wingtip smoke generators to full effect.** PRM

Above: A British Airways Concorde in a formation flypast with the nine Hawks of the RAF's aerobatic team the *Red Arrows*. PRM

Left: Guaranteed show-stopper at the Battle of Britain show was the 'torching' demonstration by a Royal Australian Air Force F-111C. PRM

Below: US Navy Lockheed S-3B Viking from the USS *Dwight D Eisenhower*. PRM

**Above & top: Further aerial views of the extensive static display in 1990.** PRM

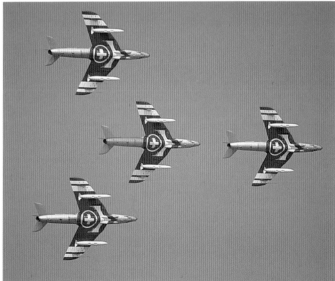

**The *Patrouille Suisse* made a welcome return with its Hunter F58s.** PRM

Around £250,000 was received by the RAFBF as a result of this successful tribute to all involved in the defence of Britain during the dark days of 1940, with more income to follow during the anniversary year including that from the *Reach for the Sky* appeal auction that September. With hindsight, the 1990 Battle of Britain Air Show also marked something of an historical turning point for IAT events, as the involvement of Czechoslovakia preceded the participation by yet more East European military metal, which was clearly evidenced back at RAF Fairford for IAT 91.

## After the Storm

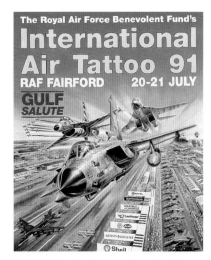

In the intervening period between the two events, much of course occurred in the world of military aviation. Operation *Desert Storm* in the Persian Gulf in early 1991 initially placed some false doubts on the coming airshow season, but these proved unfounded. RAF Fairford had been used as a base for B-52s operating bombing missions to the region, and indeed a *Gulf Salute* was a major theme of IAT 91. Additionally, the 30th Anniversary *Tiger Meet* was staged as part of proceedings, adding much colour and interest.

This was not just a meet of *Tiger Squadrons* from within NATO, as the Czechoslovak Air Force was also involved for the first time. Particularly noteworthy were the colour schemes adopted by 301 Esq, Portuguese Air Force on its Fiat G-91R, the French Mirage F1C and CM170 Magister from EC12, a Canadian CF-188 Hornet of No 439 Squadron, Belgian Air Force F-16A from 31 Smaldeel, Italian Air Force F-104S of 53 Stormo and RAF Puma, the latter No 230 Squadron aircraft gaining a Special Mention in the *Concours d'Elegance* which was won by the F-111E of USAFE's 79th TFS, one of the founder members of the Tiger Association. Four of No 74 Squadron's Phantom FGR2s represented the RAF *Tigers* in the air, with a fine formation routine.

Over 100 aircraft made up the IAT *Gulf Salute*, that again included some colourful machines. From the RAF, Tornados, Jaguar, Buccaneer, Puma, Tristar, Victor and VC10 were centres of attention for the public, but there was plenty more variety. The Italian Air Force's Tornados in their 'desert pink' liveries contrasted with the BAC 1-11 sent by the Royal Air Force of Oman, while the USAF had a range of its representative Gulf types on show. Rarest of all though were certainly the US Navy EA-3B Skywarrior and EP-3E *Aries II* Orion from VQ-2 at Rota, the former on its last outing to a UK event prior to replacement by the converted P-3s. One disappointment was the absence of an F-117, following the type's European début at Paris that June, as the 37th TFW was on call for possible further Gulf operations. A USAF B-52G flown in

**Above:** The Belgian Air Force was represented by a tiger-striped F-16A from 31 Smaldeel. GF

**Top:** This well adorned Fiat G-91R at the 1991 Tiger Meet came from 301 Esq, Portuguese Air Force. GF

**Below:** Four Phantom FGR2s from No 92 Squadron represented the RAF in the Tiger Meet, taking part in the flying display with a very tight formation routine. GF

**Aircraft on static display at Fairford in 1991 included a US Navy EA-3B Skywarrior for the last time at an IAT, and a BAC 1-11 from Oman.** PRM

by the 97th BW opened the *Gulf Salute* flying displays, that (eventually) ended with a 7th SOS MC-130E *Combat Talon I* Hercules demonstrating the Fulton recovery system, though this took some doing due to various operational difficulties!

The Czechoslovak Air Force delegation naturally caused a great stir over the weekend, with two each of 11 SLP's MiG-29As and L-39ZA Albatros plus single examples of the MiG-23ML, Tu-134A and An-12BP in attendance. The former two types flew in the display, Col Vaclav Vasek putting the *Fulcrum* through its paces in superb fashion, but sadly he suffered a technical problem on the Sunday that prevented him from

**Participants from the Czechoslovak Air Force in 1991 included a Tu-134A (right), MiG-29A, MiG-23ML and L-39ZA Albatros (below).** PRM/GF

Contrasting participants at IAT 91 included the Swiss Air Force *Tigers* flying F-5E Tiger IIs (top) and several French Air Force Fouga Magisters (below). GF

Right: Banking sharply after taking-off for his display, a French Air Force Mirage 2000. PRM

Luftwaffe Antonov An-26 *Curl* 52+07 acted as a support aircraft for the German participants at IAT 91. GF

being a contender in the flying awards. These went to Capt Reinder Zwaart in the Dutch F-16A (*International Display Sword*), Sqn Ldr Ian MacDonald of No 233 OCU flying the RAF Harrier GR5 (*Superkings Trophy*) and French Air Force Mirage 2000 pilot Capt Laurent Fournier (*Sir Douglas Bader Trophy*).

In an outstanding programme, however, there were plenty more notable items – the Swiss Air Force *Tigers* F-5E duo from FlSt 11, Spanish Air Force EF/A-18A Hornet of Ala 15 and an in-service Italian Air Force AMX operated by the RSV making their débuts; the appearance of an ex-Interflug Ilyushin Il-18 giving a pleasure flight; the Hunter's 40th anniversary, marked by a solo GA11 from the RN FRADU and the specially-painted *Patrouille Suisse* F58s, and the other

**Below: Blue-painted RAF Phantom FGR2s from Nos 56 & 92 Sqns departing from Fairford after the show.** GF

**Above: 'Gulf Salute' line-up of RAF Tornado GR1/1As and F3s.** PRM

**Propliners at IAT 91 included an ex-Interflug Ilyushin Il-18 airliner(above) operating a charter flight and Air Atlantique's DC-6 G-SIXC (inset).** GF/PRM

**Some of the larger static aircraft at IAT 91 seen from the air, dominated by a USAF C-5B Galaxy.** PRM

display teams, among them the *Frecce Tricolori* making an outstanding return and *La Patrouille ECCO*, rising from the ashes of the *Martini* trio with an excellent four-ship Pilatus PC-7 routine. Yet again, the RAFBF benefited enormously from the Tattoo, which had been enjoyed by a huge and enthusiastic audience. It was announced over the IAT 91 weekend that A&AEE Boscombe Down would again be the setting of the 'even year' event in 1992, and once more the visit to this fine airfield was eagerly awaited by many.

## Back to Boscombe

It was once again a full-scale IAT event that was presented at the MoD(PE) airfield, entitled Air Tournament International 92 and blessed with perfect weather – hot and sunny for arrivals, rehearsals, the display days on 13-14 June, and departures. There were more 'firsts' at ATI than ever before, many from the East Europeans that for the first time at any IAT display included the

**The dramatic arrival at Boscombe of the Russian Su-27P *Flanker* and Tu-134 support aircraft.** R L WARD

Russians. Certainly, the foremost memory for those who attended was the arrival direct from its home base on the Saturday of renowned test pilot Anatoly Kvotchur in his Su-27P *Flanker* from the LII Gromov Flight Research Institute at Zhukovsky. As all who attended will surely recall, he flew low and slow down the runway alongside his support Tu-134 before pulling up into his routine – the first of Kvotchur's many UK appearances flying this large interceptor.

The Czechs this time flew in an An-12, pairs of L-39ZAs and MiG-29As from 11 SLP, a 30 BILP Su-25K and Su-22M4 from 20 SBOLP – the latter two types never previously seen at an airshow in this country. The Albatros and *Fulcrum*, again flown by Vaclav Vasek, were

**First timer at Boscombe was a RNZAF MB339CB (top) whilst Vulcan B2 XH558 (above) made its last IAT appearance.** GF/PRM

joined on the programme by the specially-painted Su-25K *Frogfoot* that replaced the listed MiG-21, the type having been grounded after a fatal accident back home. The fast jet displays were of a particularly high standard at ATI, with the RAF Phantom (in its last display season), French Navy Super Etendard, Spanish Air Force EF/A-18A, US Navy F-14B from VF-74 off the USS *Saratoga* and all three F-16s but particularly the Norwegian example, all being most dynamic. ATI 92 saw the last appearance at an IAT show by the RAF's Vulcan B2 XH558, a sight much missed but not forgotten.

The *Patrulla Aguila* displayed a bright new colour scheme on its C-101 Aviojets, and the Swedish Air Force displayed an entirely new team for a UK event in the shape of *Team 60* and its Saab 105s.

**The Czech Su-25K *Frogfoot* (top) and Su-22M4 *Fitter* (above) were both new types at an IAT event.** GF/PRM

**Swedish Air Force *Team 60*, flying Saab 105s.** GF

Novelties such as the RNZAF MB339CB on delivery to No 14 Squadron, Nyge Aero's Zlin 242L (then being promoted by CSE Aviation for the RN/RAF EFTS Chipmunk replacement contract) and three home-based SE5a replicas of the Bustard Flying Group added to almost nine hours of flying.

The primary theme this time was the 50th anniversary of the arrival in the UK of the Eighth Air Force, USAAF. An hour of the flying display included various representative warbirds, most notably the Confederate Air Force's B-24A/LB-30B Liberator *Diamond Lil* after its troubled flight from Fort Worth, and The Fighter Collection's P-38J Lightning that had only just arrived in the UK at Ipswich Airport after restoration at Chino and its own ship-borne transatlantic voyage. The B-24 joined B-17G

**Warbirds at Boscombe included a P-38J Lightning and P-47M Thunderbolt (left) and the Confederate Air Force's LB-30B Liberator *Diamond Lil*.** GF/PRM

**Final appearance by a Lightning at an IAT event was made at Boscombe Down in 1992, by British Aerospace's F6 XS904.** GF

Above: A pair of German Air Force HFB320 Hansa trainers, in their final year of service, were welcome participants at Boscombe Down. GF

Other rare types at Boscombe Down in 1992 included Martin-Baker's ejector-seat trials Meteor (above) and a US Navy C-2A Greyhound (right). GF

*Sally B* and TFC's B-25D Mitchell in the bomber flypasts, with the P-38 Lightning tailchasing with two Spitfires, P-47M Thunderbolt, two P-51D Mustangs and BAe's restored and repainted Mosquito. After these, a low and fast USAF B-52G flypast depicted the modern 8th Air Force.

Fifty years of test flying at Boscombe Down was also marked, and trials and development aircraft in the static included Martin-Baker's modified Meteor, then seldom seen in public, and BAe Warton's superb Lightning F6 XS904, lined up next to the Czech *Fitter*. Then there were the two French Navy F-8E(FN) Crusaders from 12F, two German Air Force HFB320 Hansa ECM trainers in their last year of service with JBG-32, a Hungarian Air Force An-26, Turkish Air Force F-4Es from 7cu AJU and an E-3A Sentry from No 18 Squadron, Royal Saudi Air Force, making this at the time the most impressive international selection at

RAF participation at Boscombe Down in 1992 included a Boeing Sentry AEW1 (top) and a formation of BBMF Spitfire and Tornado F3 (above). PRM/GF

The USAF again provided a B-52 Stratofortress for the flying display. GF

any IAT. There was also more from the US Navy, with not just the Tomcat but also an S-3B Viking and F/A-18C Hornet coming from the USS *Saratoga*, plus three P-3Cs and an EP-3E, KC-130T and a C-2A – the largest ever number of USN aircraft featured at a UK event.

There was no doubt that ATI 92 broke new ground as far as UK displays were concerned. Again a huge donation was made to the Benevolent Fund, following one of the best air displays ever seen in the world and one that featured several aircraft whose presence at a display at the UK's premier flight test centre would have been unthinkable just a few years previously. East-West relations, now well-cemented, were further warmed that same year when the IAT organising team assisted the Czechoslovak Air Force in staging its International Air Fest at Bratislava-Ivanka, a collaboration which started in 1991 and has continued with both the Czech and Slovak air arms.

Unfortunately, 1992 was to be the last occasion that Boscombe Down could be used by the Tattoo team, as the logistics of switching venues in 'alternate years' from Fairford to another airfield away from IAT's headquarters were too costly.

Above: A USAF RC-135 climbs away from Boscombe Down on the Monday after the show. GF

Welcome foreign participation in 1992 included Spanish Air Force EF-18 Hornets (above) and Turkish Air Force F-4E Phantoms (inset). GF

## RAF's 75th Anniversary

International Air Tattoo 93, again at RAF Fairford, was planned from the outset as the official public celebration of the Royal Air Force's 75th anniversary. Alongside the especially large RAF participation, more foreign nations than ever brought with them more different types than ever as well, including various débutantes and some final appearances. Naturally, East Europeans were foremost, and indeed it was the Russians that hit the headlines – though, of course, partly for the wrong reason.

If test pilot Anatoly Kvotchur made a big impact with his Su-27 routine at ATI 92, then his comrades Sergei Tresvyatskii and Alexsandr Beschastnov flying a pair of MiG-29s from the Gromov Flight Research Institute made an even bigger impact at IAT 93 – quite literally. Coming

towards the end of their duo display during the Saturday programme, a join-up manoeuvre sadly went wrong, one pilot losing sight of the other, leading to a devastating mid-air collision. Both pilots ejected, the two *Fulcrums*, colourfully liveried in the striking yellow, blue and black colours of the Tzar's Air Fleet, being

The mid-air collision of the two Russian MiG-29s at Fairford in 1993 from which both pilots escaped unhurt. Terry Clements/Martin Heale

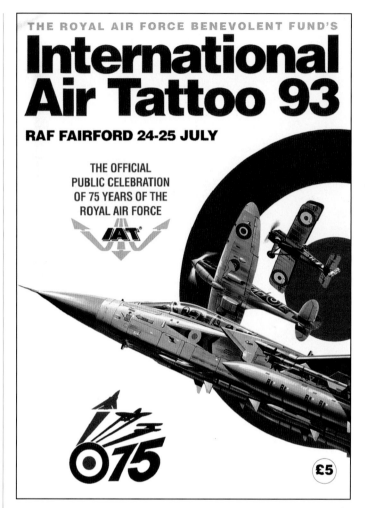

THE ROYAL AIR FORCE BENEVOLENT FUND'S
# International Air Tattoo 93
## RAF FAIRFORD 24-25 JULY

THE OFFICIAL PUBLIC CELEBRATION OF 75 YEARS OF THE ROYAL AIR FORCE

IAT

○75

£5

destroyed – one crashing outside the airfield, the other on the northern boundary fence. There was relatively minor damage to several aircraft on the north side operational aprons, the worst affected being a Belgian C-130 that lost part of its tailplane, but no-one else on or outside the airfield suffered serious injury. The flying display was able to continue almost immediately following the first serious accident in IAT's history. This all illustrated the effectiveness of IAT's Emergency Services plan, which has served as a model for other airshow organisers around the world.

Thankfully, no problems were encountered with the Russian Air Force's most significant contribution, the Tupolev Tu-95MS *Bear-H*. The 182nd Heavy Bomber Regiment at Mozdok, part of Long-Range Strategic Aviation, provided the long-awaited UK début of the type, and its flyby for the press and those in the Park and View facility with the supporting Il-78 *Midas* tanker was one of the year's most memorable

The newly-restord Blenheim IV helped celebrate the RAF's anniversary. PRM

**BAe's Mosquito RR299 evoked wartime memories.** PRM

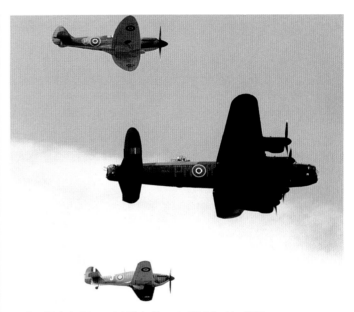

*Battle of Britain Memorial Flight* flypast at Fairford in 1993. GF

sights. On static display over the weekend, these two types looked most impressive, especially parked near to the USAF's B-1B, B-52H and KC-135s – a sight again unthinkable not many years before.

The RAF celebrations saw the Service line up most of its current types in the static park, and a 75th anniversary Pageant in the air. Shuttleworth Collection types depicted *Those Early Days*, followed by the Mosquito and the Aircraft Restoration Company's newly-restored Blenheim IV plus of course the *BBMF* Hurricane, Spitfire and Lancaster to cover the years of WW2. The modern-day section opened with the 20-ship Hawk 75' formation, not flown at the aborted Marham Royal

Review because of the inclement weather, and continued with many of the RAF's solo display aircraft and flypasts of tankers and Hercules. The finale, with Lancaster, Spitfire and Mosquito leading in the *Red Arrows* joined by a Tornado GR1A and F3 and a Harrier GR5, provided a fitting conclusion to these major and fitting celebrations.

Although rather overshadowed by the Russians, other nations made their marks on the ground and in the air. The static area featured Czech Air Force An-12 and Su-22M4, Brazilian Air Force KC-137 of 2/2 GT, the soon-to-be-retired Canberra B2 from the German Air Force's WTD-61, an IAI 1124N SeaScan of the Israeli Air Force, Kuwait Air Force

**Formation flypast by five RAF Hercules C1/C3s as part of the 75th anniversary celebrations.** GF

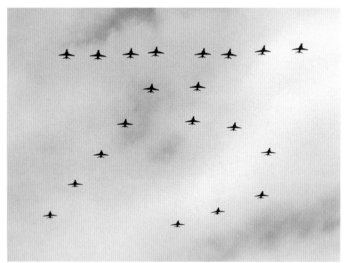

RAF Hawks in a special 75th anniversary formation. PRM

Below: Foreign aircraft at IAT 93 included Swedish Air Force JA37 Viggens and the familiar German Air Force Canberra B2 99+34. GF

Teams at IAT 93 included the Chilean Air Force *Halcones* with its new Extra 300s (top), and the MiG-21s of the *Hungarian Sky Hussars* (above). GF

L100 Hercules and F/A-18D, two colourful Fiat G-91Rs from the Portuguese Air Force shortly before their demise, a Turkish Air Force F-104G and TF-104G both from 8cu AJU among many, many others. USAF participation included an antennae-laden EC-130E from the 193rd SOS, PA ANG and, for the first time, a 56th RQS HH-60G Pavehawk based at Keflavik. A trio of USN carrier aircraft (an A-6E, F-14A and F/A-18C) this time came in from the USS *Theodore Roosevelt*.

The flying awards included the new *UK Display Sword* for the best performance by a UK military item, this going to the Army Air Corps *Silver Eagles* helicopter team of one Lynx and three Gazelles. Once again, the Chilean Air Force *Halcones* (now flying Extra EA300s) were among those taking home silverware, winning the *Sir Douglas Bader Trophy*, while the French Air Force Mirage 2000 also impressed the

Below: Brazilian Air Force KC-137 was on static display in 1993. GF

judges for a second time in order for Capt Thierry Lang to be awarded the *Superkings Trophy*. Maj Jan Frojd from F4 Wing, Swedish Air Force, pilot of the dramatic JA37 Viggen (another IAT first-timer) took away the *International Display Sword* after a fine showing.

The Hungarian Air Force *Kapos* Fighter Division flew four MiG-21bis as the *Hungarian Sky Hussars*, combining a solo pilot and combat demonstration. This was the first appearance in a UK flying programme of the type. The Czechs, aside from the solo L-39MS, MiG-29 and Su-25 displays, rather stole the limelight as well from Western air forces by

Highlight of the 1993 show was the first visit to the UK of a Russian Air Force Tu-95MS *Bear-H*, seen being escorted to Fairford by an RAF Tornado F3. RAF

Top: The *Bear* and an Il-78 *Midas* tanker gave a tanking demonstration just prior to the show. APM

Above: Distinctive shape of a USAF EC-130 on approach to Fairford. GF

Left: 1993 saw the first appearance of a IAI 1124N SeaScan of the Israeli Air Force, seen departing from the show. GF

**Above: Static display of test aircraft from Boscombe Down in 1993.** PRM

sending a display team of transport aircraft. The *Szobi Kvartet* of four L-410T Turbolets, on their inaugural UK outing, impressed all with their bomb-burst using coloured smoke. Also new was the Kuwait Air Force's No 9 Squadron *Red Hats* duo of F/A-18Cs and the Slovak Air Force L-39C team, the *Biele Albatrosy*, while the German Air Force and Navy returned to the IAT flying for the first time since 1987.

The *Royal Jordanian Falcons* brought their new Extra EA300s, and on Sunday were watched by King Hussein, who later gave a flypast in the Royal Jordanian Flight's Dove. Another welcomed display team was the first appearance by all four Stearmans of the *Cadbury's Crunchie Flying Circus*, each with a 'girl on the wing', which on Sunday flew through a torrential downpour. In spite of some poor weather over the weekend and the MiG-29s' accident, this was an enormously successful IAT. Over £300,000 was raised for the Benevolent Fund, and with this announcement came the news that the event would now be held annually at Fairford.

## Annual IAT at Fairford

Thus, the Tattoo team remained at the Gloucestershire airfield (which marked its 50th anniversary that year) for IAT 94 on 30-31 July. Poor weather again somewhat hampered the weekend at times, but there was more than enough to savour, including the 36-aircraft line of C-130 Hercules marking the type's 40th anniversary. Heading them all was *First Lady*, the AC-130A 53-3129 of AFRes that was the first production C-130A, making a return (its last) visit. The *Concours d'Elegance* winner was ski-equipped LC-130H 83-0490 of the 139th AS, New York ANG, one of the fifteen USAF *Fat Alberts* on display. Other notables included the Royal Malaysian Air Force C-130H-30, a Brazilian Air Force SC-130E and Omani C-130H, while from closer to home the Met Research Flight's W2 *Snoopy* was especially distinctive. A five-ship RAF Hercules flypast, two more C1s from Lyneham giving a paired tactical demo and a solo C-130E/Tp84 from Sweden represented the *Herky bird* in the air – an impressive anniversary celebration.

**The Slovak Air Force aerobatic team the *White Albatroses*.** GF

The Russians this time sent two *Bears* – the Navy made its début with a Tu-142M-3 *Bear-F* from its Training Regiment at Pskov in the static, while the Air Force brought another Mozdok-based Tu-95MS that gave a flypast on the Sunday. There were more East Europeans than ever before – the Czechs flew the *Szobi Kvartet* of L-410Ts once again, plus the stunning Mi-24D *Hind* pair (one in the striking *Tiger* livery) appearing here for the first time. They also brought pairs of MiG-21MFs (from the long-serving *Delta F Aerobatic Group*), L-39MS, Su-25s and Su-22M-4s, one of each appearing in the display. From the Slovaks again came the *Biele Albatrosy*, plus 1 SLP MiG-29s and MiG-21MFs for

**The Russian Navy Tu-142M-3 *Bear-F* in the static display.** GF

The 40th anniversary Hercules Meet (bottom) attracted varied examples of the type from around the world. Aircraft from the United States included a gunship AC-130A (above) and ski-equipped LC-130H of the New York ANG (below). PRM/APM/GF

static and flying. The example of the latter in the static park was presented to the RAFBF for sale. All this was an exceptionally impressive contribution by any standards.

At long last, the French Air Force supplied a beautiful Mirage IVP operated by EB1/91 for static display, while its newer counterpart, the Mirage 2000 flown by Capt Pierre Pougheon, stole the *International Display Sword* – making a hat-trick of flying prizes for this magnificent display aircraft. The Italians, *Frecce Tricolori* included, brought no fewer

**The Swedish Air Force J32 Lansen (left) and French Air Force Mirage IVP (below) were first time visitors to IAT in 1994.** PRM

**Russian Air Force Il-76 *Midas* (above) and Italian Air Force Piaggio P.180 Avanti (left) at IAT 94.** GF/PRM

than 23 aircraft, their largest-ever IAT representation, including pairs of 5 Stormo F-104S/ASAs and TF-104Gs of 4 Stormo for the static plus the familiar G222 and less well-known (but certainly distinctive) Piaggio P.180 Avanti aerobatic displays, both from the RSV. There were three Swedish Air Force J-35J Drakens present from F10, one flown by Capt Ingemar Axelsson who won the *Superkings Trophy*, and an even rarer J-32E Lansen flown in the ECM training role by F16M. The Spanish Navy's Eslla 008 flew one of its last remaining AV-8A(S) Matadors and

The Comet (above) and Hunter FGA9 (right) from the A&AEE at Boscombe Down took part in the flying display, with the Comet making a spectacular landing on the wet runway. GF

Swedish Air Force J35 Draken (left) and Spanish Navy TAV-8A and AV-8A(S) Matadors (below). GF/APM

put a TAV-8A(S) and Citation II in the static, while another unusual aircraft on the ground was the Finnish Air Force L-90TP Redigo. Of course, the *Patrouille Suisse* was present, giving its last UK display with the Hunter F58s and taking home the *Sir Douglas Bader Trophy* for good measure.

The final prizewinner was Fg Off Mark Discombe, winner of the *UK Display Sword* for his Tucano T1 performance. A&AEE/DGT&E Boscombe Down sent the Comet 4C and Hunter FGA9 for what was

stated to have been their first and last flying displays, and both were flown brilliantly. However, both have continued in service. The Royal Jordanian Air Force Historic Flight's Vampire T55 was watched for the first time by HM King Hussein, but its Hunter T7 went unserviceable. Another classic type much in evidence was British Airways Concorde G-BOAC, flying charters arranged by Goodwood Travel to celebrate the SST's 25th anniversary.

After 1993's near disaster, this was an accident-free display and one

**Let 410 Turbolets of the Czech Air Force team the *Szobi Quartet*.** JD

relatively free of operational headaches. However, a reduced crowd figure in 1994 prompted something of a rethink into the structure of the event. In amongst all of this activity, the IAT team continued its involvement overseas – an example being the assistance provided in organisation of the Slovak Air Force International Air Display at Bratislava in May 1995.

## The Victory Airshow

With much more competition now in evidence for air displays from other weekend attractions, the decision was made to restructure the flying programme for IAT 95, dividing it into themed tableaux including

specially arranged set-piece demonstrations, and the closing ceremonies to mark the 50th anniversary of the end of the Second World War.

Thankfully, the weather was excellent for the *Victory Airshow* on 22-23 July, and there was hardly a dry eye among the thousands of WW2 veterans present during the commemorative finale. This was narrated by BBC Radio Four Chief Announcer, Peter Donaldson, and had in a large part been devised by IAT's Chief Commentator, Sean Maffett. The international armada of fast jets and helicopters on and above the runway respectively were just part of this amazing piece of aerial theatre. It was opened with a flypast of a dozen vintage Tiger Moths, followed by two *Missing Man* formations of RAF and USAAF warbirds, then RAF Hawks, German Tornados and a B-1B at high speed, concluded by a Spitfire VB, P-51D Mustang and Messerschmitt Bf109G-2 flying through a smoke 'V' created by the *Red Arrows* – a truly memorable and emotional close to a spectacular flying display.

The 1995 SkyTanker meet brought together many 'flying fuel stations', including eight USAF KC-135s and types from many other nations. Among these was South Africa, with an immaculate Boeing 707-344C of No 60 Squadron being this country's first military

**Left & below: Scenes from the Victory Finale at IAT 95.** PRM/BD

The SkyTanker gathering at IAT 95 (above) included a first visit by a South African Air Force Boeing 707-344C of No 60 Squadron (below). PRM

representative ever at a UK event. Its crew enjoyed a successful visit, taking home several of the SkyTanker awards, while the organising team for the SAAF's 75th Anniversary International Military Air Show at Waterkloof also arrived aboard the 707, to gain experience that was then put to good use for the excellent event in October that was attended by Paul Bowen and a small RAFBF team. The SkyTanker line featured further rare visitors from Brazil (KC-137), Canada (KCC-130 and CC-137), Saudi Arabia (KE-3A and KC-130), Italy (B707) and France (C-135FR). RAF VC10s 'filling up' a Tristar and Harrier GR7s impressed in the air.

Fairford-based U-2Rs were operational in the days leading up to IAT. PRM

The *Hendon Heritage* pageant looked back over airshow history, with 'fort bombing' from Flycatcher, SE5a, Avro 504K, Tutor, Hind and Gladiator, WW2 warbirds and classic jets leading into more modern airshow favourites and newcomers through the British Aerospace Defence and *Best of IAT* sections. The Czech Air Force's *Akrobaticka Skupina Duha* of 321 TPZLT with its four Su-22M-4Ks and single two-seat Su-22UM-3K *Fitters* displayed dynamically, but it was the three Mi-24V *Hinds* from 331 VRLT of the same air arm that really starred, performing in

Hawk celebrations were marked with a line-up of numerous variants. PRM

Aerobatic teams at IAT 95 included the Polish Air Force *Iskras* (above) and the *Patrouille Suisse* with new F-5E Tiger IIs (below). PRM

stunning fashion and deserving winners of the *Sir Douglas Bader Trophy*. Other display teams included the brilliant *Frecce Tricolori*, a return by the Moroccan *Marche Verte*, the first UK appearance of the *Patrouille Suisse* flying F-5Es and the Polish Air Force's début in any form, flying nine PZL-Mielec TS-11 Iskras. In contrast, the Royal Netherlands Air Force *Grasshoppers* brought its Alouette IIIs for the last time, the team disbanding soon afterwards. Watched by HRH Prince Feisal of Jordan,

This Czech Air Force Antonov An-30 is operated under the 'Open Skies' agreement. PRM

**Heavy metal from Eastern Europe at IAT 95 – Slovak Air Force MiG-29A *Fulcrum* (above) and Czech Air Force Su-22M *Fitters*.** JD/BD

**Bowing out at IAT 95 were the Alouette IIIs of the Dutch *Grasshoppers* team, whilst Eurofighter 2000 (bottom) made its fleeting debut.** BD/PRM

the *Royal Jordanian Falcons* took the *Lockheed Martin Cannestra Trophy*.

IAT 95 saw the long-awaited UK public début of the Eurofighter 2000, flown gently by project pilot John Turner. Equally notable within the BAe theme in the static, marking 21 years of both the Hawk and Tornado, was a new Harrier T10 from Boscombe Down, a Tornado IDS of No 7 Squadron, Royal Saudi Air Force and Finnish Air Force Hawk Mk51A. The solo RAF Hawk, flown by Flt Lt Don Ritch of No 4 FTS, won the *UK Display Trophy*. The other prizewinner was the Slovak Air Force MiG-29 flown by Maj Ivan Hulek from 31/1 SLK, recipient of the *Superkings Trophy*, while more jet noise came from the SF37 Viggen of F7 Wing, Swedish Air Force, a German Navy Tornado and, loudest of all, the return of the USAF to the flying for the first time in a few years, courtesy of a B-1B from the 28th BS.

Adding to the *Best of IAT* selection was the international array apart from the SkyTankers in the static – Czech *Open Skies* An-30 and its DTEO Andover counterpart, the Swedish VIP Saab 340/Tp100, Italian Air Force TF-104Gs, Portuguese Air Force TA-7P, Turkish Air Force F-4Es and a former *Patrouille Suisse* Hunter F58, donated to the RAFBF and then bought by the RJAF Historic Flight. Without doubt, the IAT 95 *Victory Air Show* broke new ground as an air display spectacular, presenting not only attractions for the general public and great interest for the enthusiast but also an entirely new style of flying programme – the IAT *Theatre of the Air*. The very first Air Tattoo at North Weald back in 1971 was a standard-setting event and 25 years later the world's greatest aviation spectacular is still leading the way.

# SOLO JET DISPLAY TROPHY WINNERS
## INTERNATIONAL AIR TATTOOS 1972-1996

1972

1974

At the 1972 Embassy Air Tattoo, the second Royal Air Force Association South East Area event held at North Weald, the show's sponsor, W.D.& H.O. Wills, generously presented the Embassy Solo Jet Aerobatic Trophy, for the best display given by the pilot of a single-seat jet aircraft. The winner on that first occasion was Rod Dean, flying a Hawker Hunter from No 229 OCU at RAF Chivenor.

No longer in the RAF, Rod Dean (pictured above in 1995) is today still a regular IAT participant, flying vintage warbirds such as the Spitfire and Mustang. He hopes to return on the 25th anniversary of his award winning display, to fly a civilian Hunter at the Royal International Air Tattoo 1997.

1976

### EMBASSY JET AEROBATIC TROPHY

EMBASSY AIR TATTOO 1972
**Fg Off R. Dean – Hawker Hunter F6A, RAF**

EMBASSY AIR TATTOO 1973
**Flt Lt W. Tyndall – BAC Jet Provost T5, RAF**

EMBASSY AIR TATTOO 1974
**Flt Lt Peter Chapman – BAC Lightning F3, RAF**

INTERNATIONAL AIR TATTOO 1976
**Flt Lt David Webb – BAC Jet Provost T5, RAF**

INTERNATIONAL AIR TATTOO 1977
**Flt Lt David Fitzsimmons – HS Hawk T1, RAF**

INTERNATIONAL AIR TATTOO 1979
**Oberleutnant Wolf – Saab 105OE, Austrian Air Force**

INTERNATIONAL AIR TATTOO 1981
**Capt Hans Hemmelder – Northrop NF-5A, R Netherlands Air Force**

INTERNATIONAL AIR TATTOO 1983
**Flt Lt M. Thompson – BAC Lightning F3, RAF**

1979

# SUPERKINGS TROPHY FOR THE BEST SOLO JET DEMONSTRATION

In 1985 the parent company, Imperial Tobacco, changed the title of the award for the best single/two seat jet demonstration to the Superkings Trophy, and has since continued to present it at every Air Tattoo. The latest winner was Col Nikolai Koval from the Air Force of the Ukraine flying a Sukhoi Su-27 at The Royal International Air Tattoo.

1987

1989

INTERNATIONAL AIR TATTOO 1985
**Major Eric Nedergaard – McDonnell Douglas F-15C Eagle, USAFE**

INTERNATIONAL AIR TATTOO 1987
**Flt Lt Paul Brown – Panavia Tornado F3, RAF**

INTERNATIONAL AIR TATTOO 1989
**Flt Lt Simon Meade – HS Hawk T1A, RAF**

INTERNATIONAL AIR TATTOO 1991
**Sqn Ldr Ian MacDonald – BAe Harrier GR5, RAF**

AIR TOURNAMENT INTERNATIONAL 1992
**Cdt Dany Payeur – D-BD Alpha Jet E, Belgian Air Force**

INTERNATIONAL AIR TATTOO 1993
**Cpt Thierry Lang – Dassault Mirage 2000B, French Air Force**

INTERNATIONAL AIR TATTOO 1994
**Capt Ingemar Axelsson – Saab J-35J Draken, Swedish Air Force**

INTERNATIONAL AIR TATTOO 1995
**Maj Ivan Hulek – Mikoyan MiG-29A, Slovak Air Force**

THE ROYAL INTERNATIONAL AIR TATTOO 1996
**Col Nikolai Koval – Sukhoi Su-27A, Air Force of the Ukraine**

1993

1991

1992

1994

1995

# THE ROYAL INTERNATIONAL AIR TATTOO

## SILVER JUBILEE AIRSHOW EXCEEDS EXPECTATIONS

Of the small band of volunteers who staged the inaugural Embassy Air Tattoo and the enthusiastic crowd that attended it 25 years ago at North Weald, few could have guessed that this relatively small event would have grown into the world's premier display of military aircraft and be granted official recognition by Her Majesty The Queen. The Royal International Air Tattoo at RAF Fairford, on 20-21 July 1996 continued the traditions established in that quarter-century, of providing the very best in aerial entertainment, with over 400 aircraft participating in the flying and static displays. The celebration of IAT's Silver Jubilee enjoyed superb weather throughout the six days of arrivals, flying display weekend and departures, helping to attract more than 150,000 people to Fairford.

Some 40 air arms from 26 nations, two of them (the Irish Republic and the Ukraine) appearing for the first time, contributed to this the first Royal International Air Tattoo. The SeaSearch 96 Meet attracted some of the most notable aircraft, including the début at an airshow outside its home nation of an Ilyushin Il-38 *May*, operated by the Russian Navy's Training Regiment at Ostrov. It headed the maritime

**The South African Air Force C-130B Hercules from No 28 Squadron was the winner of the SeaSearch *Concours d'Elegance*.** APM

line-up alongside the Beriev A-40 Mermaid, representing another 'coup' for the IAT organisers. Just a few years ago, the thought of this Soviet maritime patrol aircraft appearing at an airshow in the West would have seemed ridiculous, as it was RAF interceptor crews high over the North Sea and not airshow visitors who got to see a *May* at close quarters. Accompanying the *May* and Mermaid was another welcome Russian, a twin-jet Antonov An-72A *Coaler* of Russian AF VVS Transport Aviation, making its first IAT appearance.

The SeaSearch *Concours d'Elegance* winner was the C-130B Hercules of 28 Squadron, South African AF, whose crew took home with them the Page Aerospace Trophy. This aircraft carried colourful markings applied to mark the SAAF's 75th anniversary last year. A

**Russian visitors to Fairford for the Royal International Air Tattoo SeaSearch maritime meet included a debut appearance by an Ilyushin Il-38 *May* (left) together with the experimental Beriev A-40 Mermaid (below).** APM/PRM

Special Mention, and the Evans Halshaw Trophy, went to another rare Hercules, the KC-130H from 103 Squadron of the Israeli Air Force. Unfortunately, the Royal Malaysian Air Force C-130H-MP suffered hail damage to its nose while en route to Fairford. It departed early for repairs, the crew taking with them the award for the longest distance SeaSearch visitor.

A Royal Norwegian Air Force P-3N Orion of 333 Skv joined two US Navy P-3Cs and a Canadian CP-140, while the Spanish Air Force provided an F-27-400MPA Friendship from 802 Esc – this type returning to IAT for the first time since the SeaSearch Meet in 1981. A Swedish Air Force AJSH37 Viggen made the UK début of this anti-shipping strike variant and was shown with a wide array of weapons. Also appearing for the first time was an Irish Air Corps CN235MPA Persuader, with its distinctive all-over blue livery. There were also civilians, among them a Swedish Coastguard C212 Aviocar which was Highly Commended in the fixed-wing judging, and something a little older from Air Atlantique in the shape of one of its Pollution Control C-47B Dakotas.

On the rotary wing side, a 15 Stormo AS-61R Pelican was particularly welcome from the Italian Air Force, with the Swedish Air Force also providing one of its AS332M/Hkp10 Super Pumas, likewise used for SAR duties. An SA330C Puma of 751 Esq represented the Portuguese Air Force, while an HH-60G Pavehawk from the USAF's 56th RQS made a return visit from Keflavik. The RAF Search and Rescue Training Unit provided a Wessex HC2 from Valley and it was joined by a predecessor – Austen Associates' yellow Whirlwind HAR10. In spite of strong competition, the Royal Danish Navy Lynx Mk90 was the recipient of the Cobham Trophy, having been Highly Commended in the rotary-wing section.

A short SeaSearch segment of the daily eight-hour flying

**With The Royal IAT celebrating the type's 30th anniversary, Harriers were much in evidence. Several mixed formations of T7s and T10s took part in the set-piece finale to the flying display.** BD

programme included an historical element from the RN Historic Flight's two Swordfish (only one on the Sunday), followed by an RAF Nimrod MR2 that made a couple of passes, while the Royal Netherlands Navy flew an SH-14D Lynx from 860 Squadron and a 321 Squadron P-3C-II Orion, the latter giving a very lively flying demonstration.

The Royal IAT also marked two important aircraft anniversaries this year, the most noisy of which was the celebration of 30 years of the Harrier. All four RAF squadrons flying the unique V/STOL aircraft (Nos 1, 3, 4 and 20(R) Squadrons provided examples, with a solo GR7 being backed up by no less than 10 more GR7s and T10s, which collectively provided the flying display finale. A set-piece scenario

**SeaSearch participants included an Irish Air Corps CN235MPA Persuader (left), P-3 Orions from the US Navy and Royal Norwegian Air Force plus a Canadian Forces CP-140 Aurora (below).** APM

Ray Hanna in Spitfire LFIXB MH434 led the *Red Arrows* in a formation flypast over Fairford to mark the 60th anniversary of the first flight of R.J. Mitchell's classic fighter. APM

involved a mass launch from the runway and northern taxiways, followed by an airfield attack in order to assist in the 'securing' of the airfield by troops deployed from two Hercules C1s. To follow all of this, 800 NAS provided a Sea Harrier FA2 for a solo display, prior to the return of the RAF Harriers for box-four formation flypasts and run-and-breaks to land. To close the show, a noisy hovering ballet was performed by four GR7s and T10s.

With celebrations at most events to mark the 60th anniversary of the first flight of the Supermarine Spitfire, IAT presented its own tribute to R.J. Mitchell's thoroughbred. Ray Hanna, at the controls of the Old Flying Machine Company's Spitfire LFIXB MH434, led the nine Hawks of the *Red Arrows* in a flypast, which sounded almost as special as it looked. He then pulled up into his classic aerobatic display in this most famous of all Spitfires. This was a double celebration – as Ray Hanna had flown MH434 at the very first Air Tattoo in 1971. He was also a member of the *Red Arrows* at its formation and team leader from 1966-69, making this an even more memorable occasion, leading the nine Hawks in a flypast some 30 years later.

Much of the flying display and aircraft lined up in the static parks reflected the Tattoo's international diversity. One 'first time' air arm that attracted a good deal of attention with its pair of brightly-painted Su-27A *Flankers* and supporting Il-76MD was the Air Force of the Ukraine. It enjoyed a particularly successful visit with one of the

The Turkish Air Force aerobatic team, the *Turkish Stars*, flying seven Northrop NF-5A/Bs, were welcome newcomers to Fairford. PRM

Sukhois flown by Colonel Nikolai Koval, winning the Superkings Trophy for the Best Solo Jet Demonstration.

More familiar was the Czech Air Force three-ship team of Mi-24V *Hinds* (the sole unarmed Mi-24DU trainer variant operated by the Czechs being on static as the spare) which again impressed everyone. Equally notable was the rather distinctive colour scheme on the solo MiG-21UM *Mongol*, which performed solo aerobatics, a single-seat MiG-21MF from the same unit appearing on the ground. Although the Slovak Air Force representation was reduced as the *White Albatros* team could not attend following an accident prior to departure, the solo MiG-29A flown by last year's solo jet winner Maj Ivan Hulek, gave its own noisy sequence, backed up by a static MiG-29UB and An-12.

There were of course plenty of national display teams, in spite of the loss of the Slovaks and commitments abroad depriving IAT of a couple of other regulars. The *Patrouille de France*, another performer at the first Tattoo 25 years ago, the *Patrouille Suisse* in its second season with F-5Es, and the Royal Jordanian *Falcons* all made return visits, as did the Swedish Air Force's *Team 60* with its six SAAB 105/Sk60s. The latter, led by Major Mats Lindskoog, won the Sir Douglas Bader Trophy for the Best Overall Flying Demonstration. Joining these teams for the first time in this country, was the Turkish Air Force aerobatic team, the *Turkish Stars/Turk Yildizlari* flying seven Northrop NF-5A/Bs. What was perhaps as notable about their appearance as their polished display, however, was their commentator, who received special mention at the post-show party. Broadcasting in his own unique and enthusiastic style he added a new dimension to the team's performance, rounding off his Sunday commentary by saying "The supersonic *Turkish Stars* display was produced by Uniwersal (sic) Studios, Taiwan!" He, and the team received an enthusiastic round of applause from the crowd.

Other flying display highlights included the French Air Force

The Controller of the RAF Benevolent Fund, Sir Roger Palin (centre), with personnel from the Air Force of the Ukraine in front of the Sukhoi Su-27A *Flanker* flown by Col Nikolai Koval (left), winner of the Superkings Trophy for the Best Solo Jet Demonstration. Vernon G Quaintance

Another first time visitor to the Tattoo was this Canadian Armed Forces CC-150 Polaris of No 437 Squadron. BD

A camouflaged Fokker 60U transport was amongst the large contribution from the Royal Netherlands Air Force. DJM

Jaguar E duo performing their close formation routine for which they were awarded the Lockheed Martin Cannestra Trophy for Best Display by an Overseas Participant. The French Army brought a clutch of helicopters, plus a smart TBM700 and a newly-repainted F406 Caravan II. From the German Air Force, there was plenty of noise and excitement from a Tornado IDS and F-4F Phantom II, the German Navy also flying a Tornado. The Italian Air Force contributed its aerobatic Aeritalia G222 sequence, complete with barrel roll, and also provided two F-104S/ASA Starfighters for the static, one of them in the new overall grey livery. Parked near these was an RF-4C Phantom II from the Spanish Air Force, another welcome return visitor to Fairford.

The Royal Netherlands Air Force was very well represented, with six F-16s on the airfield, plus a host of other interesting types. 334 Squadron's new C-130H-30 Hercules, Fokker 60U and McDonnell Douglas KDC-10 were among the stars of the static, none of them having been seen at a UK airshow before. One of the unit's last remaining Fokker F-27-100s was a weekend visitor. Another British airshow 'first' for the Tattoo was a Canadian Armed Forces CC-150 Polaris (Airbus A310) of 437 Squadron, one of several types carrying UN or IFOR titles, from recent service in the former Jugoslavia region.

As is customary US forces were present in strength, although there

was not a major involvement in the flying display. The 28th BW flew two B-1Bs in from Ellsworth AFB, one of them appearing in the display, while a pair of 2nd BW B-52Hs formed part of the SeaSearch line as the unit has a mine-laying role. There were plenty of transports, a C-5B Galaxy and two C-141B Starlifters being joined for the first time at an IAT by a 437th AW C-17A Globemaster III. This and the C-5 were relatively late additions to the participation list. Amongst the long list of USAF Hercules variants, the 193rd SOS, Pennsylvania Air National Guard (a regular Tattoo contributor over the years) brought one of its EC-130Es, and there was the first chance at a UK show to see a new AC-130U Hercules gunship from the 4th SOS, Air Force Special Operations Command. The US Navy and Marine Corps were joined at the last minute by the Army, with an AH-64A Apache and UH-60A Blackhawk arriving from Germany during the Saturday show.

Aside from the Jordanian *Falcons*, another impressive civilian team flying Extra EA300s was the Rover Group Aerobatic Team, leader Brian Lecomber receiving the Steedman Display Sword for the Best Display by a UK Participant on behalf of himself and team-mate Alan Wade. The new Transair Display Team of two Jet Provost T5s was an appropriate item, as 'Bob' Thompson, team manager and wingman to leader Tom Moloney, appeared with the Gemini Pair flying the type at

Dominating the static display were the USAF's heavylifters – a C-5B Galaxy and, for the first time at Fairford, a C-17A Globemaster III. PRM

Extensive static displays are always a feature at IAT – this AC-130U Spectre gunship was one of several Hercules variants provided by the USAF. PRM

the first Tattoo in 1971 and then in subsequent years. Another historic jet item came from the Royal Jordanian Air Force Historic Flight, which on Sunday sent all four of its aircraft – the Vampire FB6 and T55, Hunter T7 and F58. On a lighter display note, the Cadbury's *Crunchie Flying Circus* Super Stearman duo again joined up with the St Ivel *Utterly Butterly* Antonov An-2 as an entertaining opening novelty. Two more historic aircraft in attendance were a pair of retired RAF Chipmunk T10s, which departed during the Sunday display on the first leg of, what turned out to be an abortive, round-the-world flight.

British Airways marked 20 years of supersonic services, with Concorde G-BOAB arriving and departing several times over the weekend, operating charters for Goodwood Travel. Sadly, the audience was deprived of seeing an earlier trans-Atlantic pioneer, as the splendid Vickers Vimy replica 'G-EAOU' suffered an engine failure after take-off on Saturday which necessitated a hasty return. In an almost completely untroubled flying display, this was one of only three aircraft incidents over the weekend. A Harrier T10 had a birdstrike during Saturday's set-piece, but repairs were carried out and it

The Vimy made a brief flying appearance on the first day of the show. PRM

participated again on Sunday, while the German F-4's brake parachute failed to deploy on the second day, but it was able to stop safely.

On the logistics front, many of the traffic problems of recent years had been eased thanks to the new traffic flow system adopted by IAT and Gloucestershire Police. The high temperatures caused their own problems, with over 50 spectators being treated for heatstroke, but out of the huge crowd this was to be expected. The arena events and other ground attractions were as popular as ever, and the impressive 25th anniversary balloon meet of standard and special shape hot-air balloons, in tethered flight on the weekend mornings and flying free after the display, proved to be an excellent innovation.

The programme of private visits for distinguished guests including the Defence Secretary, The Rt Hon Michael Portillo, HRH Prince Michael of Kent and HRH The Duke of York (present for the SeaSearch events on the Friday), went ahead as planned, culminating on the second day with the presence of HRH Prince Feisal and HM Queen Noor of Jordan. Her Royal Highness spent time with the ten disabled recipients of this year's Royal IAT Flying Scholarships, partly sponsored by HM King Hussein (who was unable to attend this year), while Prince Feisal joined Paul Bowen, Tim Prince and Air Marshal Sir Denis Crowley-Milling to cut the Tattoo's Silver Jubilee cake, surrounded by many past and present IAT volunteers.

At the IAT prizegiving and party on the Sunday night, the Controller of the RAF Benevolent Fund, Air Chief Marshal Sir Roger Palin, declared that the first Royal International Air Tattoo had been a great success, with an extremely high standard of flying, superb weather and once again would result in a large donation to the RAF Benevolent Fund. Sir Roger also announced that The Royal International Air Tattoo 1997 will be staged on 19-20 July next year, and will mark the 50th anniversary of the formation of the USAF and will feature as its operational scene – Fighter 97, the world's first international fighter and air defence meet.

Europe's only professional wingwalking team, the *Cadbury's Crunchie Flying Circus* flew two of its Boeing Super Stearman biplanes in from Rendcomb Airfield north of Cirencester to make their traditional opening IAT appearance. Vic Norman, founder and team leader, and Mike Dentith were at the controls, with Tanya Gaze, and the very experienced wingwalker Helen Tempest, on the top wings. BD/PRM

Rendcomb-based AeroSuperbatics provided plenty of colour in the display, not only with the *Crunchies* but also the sedate appearance of its Polish-built Antonov An-2R, the big part of the *St Ivel Utterly Butterly Exhibition Flyers*. Matthew Hill put the powerful *Ant* through its distinctive paces on both days. BD

A flying prizewinner last year, the Slovak Air Force's Major Ivan Hulek of 1 Letka, 31 SLK at Sliac returned to put the MiG-29A *Fulcrum* through its paces. This aircraft is one of the newly-delivered examples provided by Russia, and wears the Air Force's latest air defence two-tone grey finish. Major Hulek's sequence included multiple tailslides and his distinctive version of the famous 'Cobra' manoeuvre.DJM/JD

Underlining the Rover Group's sponsorship of The Royal International Air Tattoo, the two Extra EA300s of the Firebird Aerobatics-operated *Rover Group Aerobatic Team* gave a breathtaking aerobatic display. This earned team leader Brian Lecomber and Alan Wade the award for the best demonstration by a UK participant at the event. GF/PRM

Denham-based Firebird Aerobatics duo Brian Lecomber and Alan Wade are in their second season flying the *Rover Group Aerobatic Team* Extra EA300s. Brian was presented on behalf of the team with the *Steedman Display Sword* for the Best Demonstration by a UK participant in the 1996 flying display, by Air Chief Marshal Sir Patrick Hine of BAe. PRM

The Royal Navy Historic Flight opened the SeaSearch flying displays, with its two vintage Fairey Swordfish IIs, W5856/A2A and LS326/L2, flying together on the opening day, but with only the former appearing on Sunday. Flown by Lt Phil Shaw and the RNHF's CO, Lt Cdr Graham Gell, they operated from RNAS Yeovilton. GF/Andrew Voice

The Nimrod MR2 display from the Kinloss MR Wing in the SeaSearch flying sequence was mounted from its temporary base at RAF Lossiemouth by different aircraft on the two days, XV229 on Saturday and XV227 on the Sunday. With no Nimrod on the airshow display scene this year, Flt Lt Lloyd Barrett and his crew were limited to making sedate role-demonstration flypasts. GF

An unusually spirited flying display was provided by the Royal Netherlands Navy's Lockheed P-3C Orion, flown by a crew from 321 Squadron based at Valkenburg. This unit, along with 320 Squadron and No 1 Maritime OTU, forms the Maritime Patrouillegroep (MARPAT), whose Orions are now in the Update II configuration. The aircraft performed steep turns, wingovers and climbouts and made a pass to show an underside view with its weapons bay open. BD/JD

Joining the Dutch Orion in the SeaSearch flying display was a Westland SH-14D Lynx operated by 860 Squadron of the Royal Netherlands Navy from De Kooy. It gave an entertaining SAR demonstration. The improved SH-14Ds of 7 and 860 Squadrons have uprated Rolls-Royce Gem 42 powerplants compared with earlier variants, and several other enhancements including the addition of GPS, RWRs and FLIR. JD

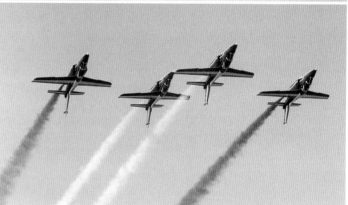

A Special Mention in the flying display awards ceremony was given to the outstanding performance by the French national aerobatic team *La Patrouille de France*. It was appropriate that the team should make its distinctive appearance this year as, then flying Fouga Magisters, it opened the main flying display at the first Tattoo at North Weald 25 years ago. Led by Major William Kurtz, in his second season as *Athos 1*, *La Patrouille de France* and its eight Alpha Jet Es are based at Salon de Provence as part of Groupement d'Instruction 00.312. All of the pilots are volunteers from front-line combat wings, who train with the *Patrouille* between November and April each year. PRM/DJM

The first visit of the Air Force of the Ukraine to a British airshow was very successful. The brightly-painted Sukhoi Su-27A *Flanker*, operated by 831 IAP (Fighter Aviation Regiment) at Mirgorod, was flown by Col Nikolai Koval through an outstanding aerobatic sequence. Not surprisingly it featured tailslides and the tight, noisy manoeuvring for which this big interceptor is known. This skilled and entertaining display won Col Koval the *Superkings Trophy*, presented by Graham Blashill of Imperial Tobacco, for the Best Solo Jet Demonstration. Peter Schenk/PRM/BSS

The *Royal Jordanian Falcons* gave their customarily polished routine in four Extra EA300s, led by Omar Hewaij. His team-mates were Qusay Zaza, Taiseer Daboubi and Omar Bilal, the latter again flying an incredible solo sequence. The team's fine aerobatics have been enjoyed on many occasions at IATs since their UK début at Greenham Common in 1979, then flying Pitts S-2s. GF/PRM

Captain Ries Kampermans, in his second season as the Royal Netherlands Air Force's solo F-16A Fighting Falcon display pilot, put on a fine demonstration again at Fairford in his colourful aircraft, J-508, equipped with wing-tip Smokewinders. The Dutch F-16 display this year is a joint effort between Volkel-based Nos 306 and 311 Squadrons. Surprisingly this was the only Fighting Falcon in the IAT flying programme this year. APM

For the second year running, the IAT crowd thrilled to the sight of three Mil Mi-24V *Hinds* from 331.vrlt of the Czech Air Force at Prerov, displaying in dramatic fashion. Led again by Lt Col Stefan Jasso, the *Skupina Mi-24* performed low-level flypasts with smoke on, fired flares and executed a very precise *Balet vrtulniku* (Helicopter ballet) with two of the *Hinds* giving an immaculate demonstration of the 'carousel' manoeuvre. DJM/BD/PRM/APM

There was a welcome return to the IAT flying display from a Luftwaffe F-4F Phantom, 37+78 of JG-71, the *Richthofen Geschwader* based at Wittmundhaven. This was one of only three aircraft over the weekend to suffer any kind of problem, when its braking parachute failed to deploy on landing on the Sunday, requiring the use of wheel brakes and a 'cooling off' period at the end of the runway. APM/GF

Marking 20 years of successful and safe supersonic passenger carrying, British Airways Concorde G-BOAB operated charter flights for Goodwood Travel on both days of the show. Here it is taking off during the flying display for a supersonic flight over the Bay of Biscay. DJM

First seen in the UK at Air Tournament International 92 at Boscombe Down, *Team 60* of the Swedish Air Force again provided a polished performance in its six SAAB 105/Sk60s. Led by Major Mats Lindskoog, the team is drawn from F5 at Ljungbyhed, with all the pilots being flying instructors within the Wing. Since that inaugural showing at ATI, the aircraft have received prominent Flygvapnet titling on their upper wing surfaces. A fine showing was rewarded with the award to Major Lindskoog on behalf of the team of the *Sir Douglas Bader Trophy*, sponsored by Shell (UK) Oil and presented by Controller of the RAF Benevolent Fund, Sir Roger Palin, for the Best Overall Flying Demonstration. DJM/BSS/GF/PRM

The French Air Force's pair of two-seat Jaguar Es made its long-awaited IAT début at an IAT this year. Contributed by Escadron de Chasse 02.007 'Argonne' from St Dizier-Robinson, this is one of the Armee de l'Air's *Bravo* display teams, which comprises two front-line fast jets performing a very close formation routine. Their sequence at Fairford was very polished, winning pilots Lt Praud and Lt Boutron the *Lockheed Martin Cannestra Trophy* for the Best Flying Demonstration by an Overseas Participant. They were presented with the award by Ken Cannestra, of long-term IAT sponsor Lockheed Martin, after whom the trophy is named. Peter Schenk/BD/BSS

The German Air Force's solo Tornado IDS display came from JBG-38 at Jever. Originally scheduled to fly only on the Saturday and to be replaced by its Marineflieger counterpart the following day, this aircraft in fact replaced the sick Vickers Vimy replica in the Sunday flying programme. APM/DJM

The German Navy Tornado IDS, 45+59 from MFG-2 at Eggebek, was only displayed on the second day. The sequence flown included an impressively short stop using reverse thrust followed by an equally short take-off. The Marineflieger's Tornado is operated in the anti-shipping role for which it is fitted with Kormoran or HARM missiles. GF

SWISS AIR FORCE TEAM
PATROUILLE SUISSE

1996 is the second season for the Swiss Air Force aerobatic team, the *Patrouille Suisse*, with its 'new' F-5E Tiger IIs. The team flew Hunters until 1994, having made its début at IAT 79 at Greenham Common, and appeared regularly at subsequent air tattoos over the next 15 years. The 1996 team leader is once again Major Frans Ramseier.

Keith Griffiths/PRM/D W Richards

In his first year as the RAF's Harrier GR7 display pilot, Flt Lt Gary Waterfall, a Weapons Instructor with No 20(R) Squadron, the Harrier OCU at RAF Wittering, helped to celebrate the 30th anniversary with his stylish routine. It was sadly cut short on the Saturday due to technical problems. Gary will continue on the display circuit next year, but as a member of the *Red Arrows*. BD

An interesting addition to the flying programme on Sunday was the departure of two Chipmunk T10s, WP833 and WP962, en route to Manston on the first leg of a planned round-the-world flight to mark the 50th anniversary of the famous trainer's first flight and its retirement from RAF service. Before their departure, Prince Michael of Kent and Prince Feisal of Jordan discussed the flight with the pilots. Sqn Ldrs Tony Cowan and Ced Hughes (the former CO of No 5 Air Experience Flight at Cambridge) were at the controls, with the other two pilots involved, Flt Lt David McKenna and Sqn Ldr Bill Purchase, following in the support Jetstream, XX492. Sadly, forest fires in Russia under the intended route caused the flight to be aborted during the first week in August. APM/DJM/PRM/BD

MBB BO105DBS/4 G-PASG, operated by Police Aviation Services for the Gloucestershire Ambulance Service NHS Trust, also acted as the customary cameraship during the display. The air-to-ground photographs used in this book were taken during the weekend sorties along the crowd line and to the south of the airfield. DJM

The Army Air Corps was once again represented in the display by the *Blue Eagles* helicopter display team from Middle Wallop. Four Gazelle AH1s and a Lynx AH7 gave a very lively and well-co-ordinated sequence. Led by Major John Davies, the routine naturally included the impressive back-flip from the Lynx that has become the AAC team's trademark. J R Hadland/DJM

The colourful RAF Valley livery worn by Hawk T1 XX235 has been carried over from last year, although the 1996 solo routine by the type is provided by No 74(R) Squadron, the *Tigers* from No 4 FTS. Flt Lt Bill Auckland, the new display pilot this year, is a Qualified Flying and Tactics Instructor with the unit and was the manager for last season's Hawk displays. PRM

Coming from No 1 Parachute Training School at nearby RAF Brize Norton, the RAF *Falcons* Parachute Display Team jumped out of a Hercules to make its colourful descent. The team, now in its 32nd season, appeared at the first Air Tattoo at North Weald in 1971, jumping from an Argosy transport, a type known as the 'Whistling Wheelbarrow'. APM

Concorde landed back at Fairford during the flying display after its 'supersonic dash'. On Saturday, the supersonic transport was flown by Captain Jeremy Randall, who was making his last flight as a Concorde pilot with the airline.
Peter Schenk

The new *Transair Display Team* with two Jet Provost T5s represented a type that has featured in almost every Air Tattoo flying programme for the past 25 years, including a number of well-known RAF formation teams. The prototype Jet Provost T5 (formerly XS230, now G-VIVM) and an ex-RAF T5A (G-BWEB, previously XW422) are used for the sequence which is new this year. Tom Moloney, founder of Transair (UK) Ltd, leads the North Weald based pair, with Bob Thompson, a very experienced JP display pilot, as No 2. Bob flew with two of the RAF's JP teams - the *Gemini Pair* from No 3 FTS (including an appearance in 1971 at the first Air Tattoo at North Weald, and No 1 FTS' *Swords* four-ship. GF/APM/PRM

The latest in a long string of aerobatic teams making their UK debuts at an IAT was the Turkish Air Force *Turk Yildizlari (Turkish Stars)* flying seven NF-5A/B Freedom Fighters. The team brought nine single-seat NF-5As and a single NF-5B two-seater to Fairford. The former Royal Netherlands Air Force aircraft, flew in via Brize Norton from their base at Konya, supported by a pair of C160 Transalls. The team gave a polished routine with some very original elements, made all the more entertaining by the lively commentary from the team's manager.

Elizabeth Braznell/Brian Brown/Peter Schenk/APM

Having made it from England to Australia in 1994, in an epic 15,000-mile, two-month flight in tribute to that made by Ross and Keith Smith 75 years before, the Vickers FB27A Vimy IV replica 'G-EAOU' (NX71MY) sadly failed in its attempt to display for the IAT audience. Ken Snell, a BA Concorde captain, got airborne on the Saturday, but suffered the failure of one of its Chevrolet V8 engines and made a careful circuit and emergency landing. The aircraft, named *Shell Spirit of Brooklands*, is currently based at Farnborough. APM/BD/DJM/BSS

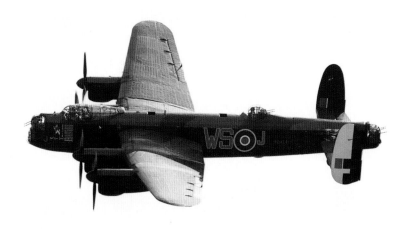

Having provided aircraft for almost every air tattoo since 1971, the Battle of Britain Memorial Flight flew Lancaster BI PA474, Hurricane IIC PZ865 and Spitfire IIA P7350 in from its base at RAF Coningsby on the opening day. Prior to this season, the Lancaster underwent an eight month re-sparring and major servicing programme, returning to the air at RAF St Athan in May. It is hoped that this work will enable it to fly on for another 50 years. JD/PRM/GF

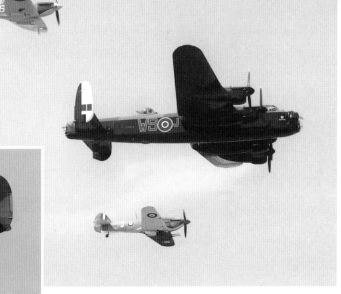

The fourth aircraft in the Battle of Britain Memorial Flight's contribution was Dakota C3, ZA947/YS-DM. Service with the RAE at West Freugh (as KG661) was followed between 1978 and 1993 by sterling work for the Farnborough-based Air Transport Flight, but when the unit was disbanded the aircraft was passed on to the BBMF. It is flown as a tailwheel conversion trainer for the Lancaster, in support of the Flight and for displays in its own right. It is painted as the aircraft in which David Lord won his posthumous VC at Arnhem. PRM

The Royal Jordanian Air Force Historic Flight provided all four of its classic jets during Sunday's programme. Vampire FB6 G-BVPO and Hunter F58 G-BWKA (formerly J-4075, a *Patrouille Suisse* aircraft) which were flown on the first day by Dick Hadlow and Brian Henwood were augmented for their second appearance of the weekend by the Flight's original two aircraft, the Vampire T55 G-BVLM and well-known Hunter T7 G-BOOM. This is the world's only national all-jet historic flight, formed under the guidance of HM King Hussein in 1994 and operated by RV Aviation and Jet Heritage. It was announced in August that the Flight was to move to Jordan in September, whereupon it will be further expanded with Royal Jordanian Air Force jets as they are retired, in the future. BSS/PRM/GF/Keith Griffiths

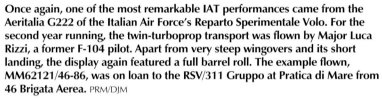

Once again, one of the most remarkable IAT performances came from the Aeritalia G222 of the Italian Air Force's Reparto Sperimentale Volo. For the second year running, the twin-turboprop transport was flown by Major Luca Rizzi, a former F-104 pilot. Apart from very steep wingovers and its short landing, the display again featured a full barrel roll. The example flown, MM62121/46-86, was on loan to the RSV/311 Gruppo at Pratica di Mare from 46 Brigata Aerea. PRM/DJM

As with many of the other RAF fast jet display aircraft, grey is the colour for the solo Tornado GR1 this year, which again comes from the Standards Squadron of the Tri-National Tornado Training Establishment at RAF Cottesmore. This scheme has provided a very smart aircraft for Flt Lt Mike Bavistock and navigator Sqn Ldr Robbie Stewart, embellished by the unit's badge and the emblem of the County of Rutland on the fin. The smartly-liveried RAF TTTE Tornado was, however, only seen on the Sunday, as the display crew from Cottesmore flew the 'spare' IDS 43+25/G-75 from the unit's German element on the first day.

JD/DJM/Mark Schenk

As last year, the 37th Bomb Squadron of the 28th BW, Air Combat Command, at Ellsworth AFB, represented the USAF in the flying display. It again fell to B-1B Lancer 85-0084/EL, named *Brute Force*, to provide the impressive flypasts. This squadron was already familiar with RAF Fairford, having been based there earlier this year on exercise. APM/Chris Mifsud

One aircraft which does not need a special display colour scheme is the Royal Netherlands Air Force's Pilatus PC-7 Turbotrainer. Capt Pieter Vrieling and his yellow painted aircraft came from the Elementaire Militaire Vlieg Opleiding (EMVO), based at Woensdrecht, that flies ten such aircraft. Both prospective rotary- and fixed-wing pilots receive basic training on the PC-7s, the former continuing on the type for more advanced instruction while those who opt for the fast jet route depart to ENJPT at Sheppard AFB, Texas. BD/JD

Yet another RAF fast jet showing off a new grey livery was the solo Jaguar GR1A from No 16(R) Squadron at RAF Lossiemouth. At the end of the season, Flt Lt Andy Cubin, the display pilot since 1994 and a Jaguar QFI, will swap from training pilots on the type for a tour with the *Red Arrows*.
APM/PRM

Having been anticipated at Fairford for the past two years, the imaginatively-painted MiG-21UM *Mongol* 3756 from the Letecki Zkusebni Odbor (LZO) based at Line appeared this year in the IAT flying programme. Flown by Lt Col Frantisek 'Frankie' Hlavinicka, a MiG-21 display pilot for 13 years with the Czech test centre, the aircraft's brickwork paintwork and wood-effect nosecone, amongst other features, made for an interesting sight. The *Stress Team* titling reflects the work carried out by the LZO investigating aircraft stresses. John Chase

Although its impressive flying appearance at IAT two years ago was billed as its last airshow outing, Comet 4C XS235 *Canopus* from DTEO Boscombe Down has continued in service, and was again described as being on show for the final time as it executed a fine display again this year. It was flown by a crew from the Heavy Aircraft Test Squadron of the Assessment & Evaluation Centre, and was put through its paces in fine style. The routine from this, the last flying DH106 anywhere in the world, included several steep wingovers, reflecting the fact that, while *Canopus* may now be 33 years old, it remains a low-houred aeroplane. PRM/JD

At the first North Weald Air Tattoo in 1971, Ray Hanna performed an exhilarating aerobatic sequence flying Supermarine Spitfire LFIXC MH434. At IAT 96, he repeated this performance, marking both the Tattoo's Silver Jubilee and the classic fighter's Diamond Jubilee. As a celebration of these anniversaries, Ray preceded his timeless demonstration of R.J.Mitchell's machine with one of the 1996 airshow season's most memorable sights – leading a flypast in close formation with the nine Hawks of the *Red Arrows*, the team that Ray Hanna himself led from 1966 to 1969. The aircraft is of course now owned by the Duxford-based Old Flying Machine Company headed by Ray and his son Mark, having in 1971 been the property of Sir Adrian Swire. The Spitfire appeared again this year in the markings, coded ZD-B and named *Mylcraine*, it wore when operated by No 222 (Natal) Squadron during WW2. DJM/PRM/APM

The RAF Aerobatic Team the *Red Arrows* has had its busiest eighteen months ever, with extended overseas tours through last winter and a mid-season tour of the Far East in support of the British aerospace industry's sales efforts in this important marketplace. However, The Royal International Air Tattoo was able to welcome the *Reds* following their return less than a week before. The team displayed after its flypast with Ray Hanna in Spitfire MH434 and his subsequent solo routine. New on the *Arrows'* roster this year are Flt Lt Andy Offer, the 1995 Harrier GR7 display pilot, and 1994's solo Hawk pilot, Flt Lt Dave Stobie. The team was led through its immaculate and varied routine by Sqn Ldr John Rands in his third and final year as *Red One*. A Dowden/GF

## 30TH ANNIVERSARY OF THE HARRIER

On 3 August 1966 the Hawker Siddeley P.1127(RAF) XV276, the first of a Development Batch of Harriers for the RAF, took off from the company's airfield at Dunsfold, to prelude a new era in the RAF's history. Since then, in a variety of guises, the classic V/STOL fighter-strike aircraft has served the RAF, and subsequently the Royal Navy and overseas operators, in its own distinctive way. The Harrier's combat service with the RAF and RN in the Falklands, and the US Marine Corps during the Gulf conflict, is legendary. It was therefore appropriate for The Royal International Air Tattoo to celebrate the 30th anniversary of the first flight of the very first Harrier, with a spectacular demonstration of the type's unique qualities.

Ten of the RAF's latest Harrier GR7s and T10s were provided by all four units operational on the type - Nos 1 and 20(R) Squadrons at Wittering and Laarbruch-based Nos 3 and 4 Squadrons - for a set-piece which concluded both days' flying programmes. Following a very noisy mass launch from different directions off the runway and the north side taxiways, the full scenario unfolded.

It involved the 're-capture' of the airfield from 'infidels', eight of the Harriers providing air support (complete with impressive pyrotechnics accompanying the airfield attack runs) which allowed a pair of Hercules from the Lyneham Transport Wing to land and offload their 'friendly' troops. The Harriers then flew past in two celebratory box-four formations. The closing 'act' further illustrated the Harrier's special qualities. A hovering aerial ballet was performed by four of the aircraft. JD/APM/PRM/Mark Schenk/André Fraiture

Left: Representing the Royal Navy's V/STOL capability as part of this Harrier anniversary tribute was Sea Harrier FA2 ZH798. It was flown by Lt Rod Player from 899 Naval Air Squadron at RNAS Yeovilton, although his aircraft was from 800 NAS. With the Blue Vixen radar and other improvements, the FA2s (either converted FRS1s or, in the case of the display aircraft, new-build machines) are highly capable air defenders. GF

## IAT SILVER JUBILEE BALLOON MEET

Extra entertainment before and after the flying displays at The Royal International Air Tattoo was provided by a large gathering of standard and special-shape hot-air balloons. A total of 28 balloons was present over the weekend, the 'meet' being under the direction of the IAT Balloon Master, Ian Cheese. Inflation took place on the far south side of the airfield for tethered flight during the morning prior to the display on both days. On Saturday evening, the weather conditions were favourable enough to allow free flight by a good proportion of the balloons, providing an interesting diversion for those who stayed on into the early evening before travelling home.

Flying Pictures, one of the UK's biggest commercial balloon operators, provided a large contingent including the new Cameron Samsung computer and the Budweiser beer can. The Chubb Fire Extinguisher came from a local Gloucestershire organisation, Cotswold Balloons from nearby Ampney St Peter. It was flown by John Albury, one of Britain's most experienced balloon pilots with over 2800 'hot air' flying hours to his name, in over 150 different balloons. John acted as the British Balloon and Airship Club's Safety Officer at IAT's Silver Jubilee Balloon Meet. Other notable special shapes included the Nestle Mug and the National Power Electricity Pylon, *Pete the Pylon*.

Naturally, Flying Pictures' Rover balloon was foremost among the standard designs, other sponsoring companies including the Royal Mail, Bath City Council and Bowyer's Pork Farms, amongst many more. Here is a selection of the hot-air balloons, some tethered and others flying free at Fairford. BD/APM/DJM/PRM

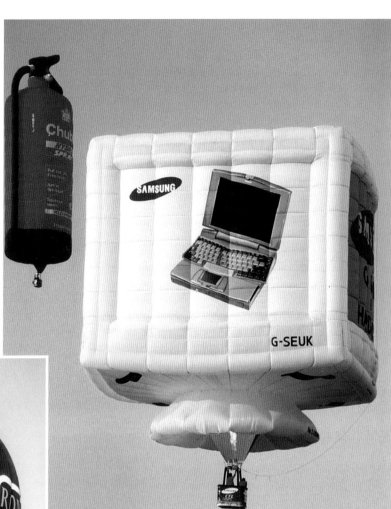

## SeaSearch 96

International Air Tattoo organised its first SeaSearch Meet at Greenham Common in 1981. It attracted an impressive gathering of maritime patrol, reconnaissance, search and rescue, anti-submarine warfare and similar aircraft from several nations. This was repeated on a bigger scale in 1989, and at this year's Royal International Air Tattoo the SeaSearch 96 gathering was the principal 'operational' theme of the event. Aircraft from 22 air arms representing 17 nations took part, including the first participation by Russia in SeaSearch and the first appearance of the Irish Air Corps with a CN235MPA, at any IAT display.

It was the Russian Navy that provided one of the Meet's highlights, sending an Ilyushin Il-38 *May* from its Training Regiment at Ostrov to make the type's début at an air display outside of the former Eastern Bloc. It was joined by the still experimental Beriev A-40 *Mermaid*, from the Design Bureau at Taganrog. The list of prizewinners below illustrates the international diversity of SeaSearch. Amongst the less familiar sights was a South African Air Force C-130B Hercules and an Israeli Air Force KC-130H, both of which took home awards. The helicopter static display also featured some uncommon types, notably an Italian Air Force AS-61R Pelican and an SA330 Puma from the Portuguese Air Force, while additionally there were interesting civilian contributions such as the Swedish Coastguard C212 Aviocar and UK Coastguard Islander. The SeaSearch theme was also reflected in the flying programme, with the RN Historic Flight's Swordfish, RAF Nimrod, Royal Netherlands Navy P-3C Orion and SH-14D Lynx taking part.

The Meet began on Thursday 18 July with a Symposium, sponsored by Lockheed Martin, at the Queen Elizabeth II Conference Centre in London. Delegates heard an international team of speakers, who presented papers on aspects of maritime aviation relating to modern maritime patrol and SAR operations. The ground competitions were held at a nearby water park during the following day, while back at Fairford aircraft were inspected by the *Concours d'Elegance* judges. The SeaSearch awards were presented on the Friday evening at the IAT 96 Gala Dinner hosted by British Aerospace. Over the weekend, crews were by their aircraft in the static park to answer questions on maritime operations from the visiting public. Some very impressive displays were mounted by individual participants in front of their aircraft, illustrating the range of equipment now used for maritime reconnaissance and SAR duties.

DJM

Brian W Brown

The SeaSearch 96 trophies and winners at The Royal International Air Tattoo were:

**Dowty Trophy** for crew travelling the greatest distance to attend: 4 Squadron, Royal Malaysian Air Force

**Rolls-Royce Trophy** for Best Recognition Skills: 7 Squadron, Royal Netherlands Navy

**Marshall Aerospace Trophy** for Best Fieldcraft: 2/1 GTT, Brazilian Air Force

**Lockheed Martin Trophy** for Best Aircrew Survival Skills: The Tweety Team – SAR Flight, Royal Netherlands Air Force

**Boeing Trophy** for Best Ground Exercise by an Overseas Crew: No 405 Squadron, Canadian Armed Forces

**British Aerospace Defence Trophy** for Best Ground Exercise by a UK Crew: No 120 Squadron, RAF

**McDonnell Douglas Trophy** for Overall Ground Competition Winners: 845 Naval Air Squadron, Royal Navy

**Lockheed Martin Tactical Systems (UK) Trophy** for *Concours d'Elegance* – Highly Commended, Fixed Wing: CASA C212 Aviocar, Swedish Coastguard

**Cobham Trophy** for *Concours d'Elegance* – Highly Commended, Rotary Wing: Lynx Mk90, Royal Danish Navy Esk 722

**Evans Halshaw Trophy** for *Concours d'Elegance* – Special Mention: KC-130H Hercules, 103 Squadron, Israeli Air Force

**Page Aerospace Trophy** for *Concours d'Elegance* – Overall Winner: C-130B Hercules, 28 Squadron, South African Air Force

**Graviner Trophy** for Spirit of the Meet: 2/1 GTT, Brazilian Air Force

PRM

# SEASEARCH 96

Heading the main SeaSearch line was a pair of Nimrod MR2s from the RAF Kinloss MR Wing. XV231 was provided by No 206 Squadron, with XV232 coming from No 201. Due to runway resurfacing at RAF Kinloss, the Wing has been deployed this year to Lossiemouth. PRM

This was possibly the last time that a yellow-painted Wessex HC2 flown in the search-and-rescue role will be seen at IAT. The Search and Rescue Training Unit at RAF Valley, which sent XV724 to Fairford for SeaSearch and No 22 Squadron, also based at Valley, are now the only users of yellow-painted SAR Wessex. JD

A SeaSearch contribution from the Royal Navy was this Lynx HAS3S, XZ698 operated by 815 NAS. The Portland-based Lynx squadrons will eventually be fully equipped with conversions to HMA8 standard, modifications including new rotor systems, upgraded thermal imaging equipment and magnetic anomaly detectors. HRH The Duke of York arrived in this helicopter on the Friday. BD

Three Sea Kings of the Royal Navy were sent to the Air Tattoo for the SeaSearch meet. HAS6 XV665 came from 810 Naval Air Squadron at RNAS Culdrose, being joined by search-and-rescue HAR5 ZA167 of 771 NAS also from the Cornish Station and commando HC4 ZD480 of Yeovilton-based 845 NAS. The latter unit currently has two aircraft each at Divulje Barracks in Croatia and Gornji-Vakuf in Bosnia, supporting the UN IFOR troops, and the example shown indeed wore the distinctive colours applied for this service. Its crew won the McDonnell Douglas Trophy as overall winners of the SeaSearch ground competition.
Kev Storer/GF

Below: Once again, the Brazilian Air Force supported the Air Tattoo with C-130H Hercules 2465 of 2 Esquadra, 1 Grupo de Transporte de Tropas at BA dos Afonsos near Rio de Janeiro. This aircraft joined the SeaSearch line by virtue of its SAR role. APM

Representing the Canadian Armed Forces in the SeaSearch line was CP-140 Aurora 140113, from No 405 Squadron of 14 Wing at Greenwood on the East Coast. The Aurora is unique in combining the P-3 Orion airframe with S-3 Viking avionics. Eighteen standard examples are operated by the Canadians with those stationed at Greenwood being augmented by examples at Comox.
PRM

Gulfstream III F-313 was, at the time of its show appearance, one of three flown by Eskadrille 721 of the Royal Danish Air Force at Vaerlose. However, the total has since decreased to two, with the tragic loss of one of the fleet in the first week in August. They were delivered in 1981-82, and are equipped with quickly-adaptable interiors enabling use for SAR and fishery protection patrols (one aircraft normally being deployed to Greenland) and communications alongside 721's transport duties, for which they are augmented by C-130s. DJM

Esk 722 at Vaerlose is a joint Royal Danish Air Force/Navy unit, its eight Sikorsky S-61As belonging to the Air Force component. They are flown on long-range SAR missions, being without any ASW equipment. For this purpose detachments are maintained at Aalborg, Ronne and Skyrdstrup. BSS/PRM

From the Naval section of Esk 722 came Lynx Mk90 S-256, a new-build example of the variant with one other older Mk 80 having already been converted to this standard and the other seven awaiting modification. Flown from shore bases and naval vessels, the Danish Lynx are used for fishery protection around the Faroe Islands and Greenland. The Mk 90 upgrade involves the installation of Kestrel ESM tactical data systems and R-R Gem 42 engines. This aircraft was the recipient of the Cobham Trophy, being Highly Commended in the Rotary Wing section of the SeaSearch *Concours d'Elegance*. Rob Holder

**Above:** This Falcon 10(MER), 143, was from 57S at Landivisiau where it is flown on training and communications duties. PRM

**Left:** The SA321G Super Frelon, 162 from 32 Flotille at Lanveoc, displayed the smart two-tone colour scheme currently being adopted on the French Navy's fleet of 18 examples of this SAR and transport helicopter. P J Hall

The German Navy's Br1150 Atlantics have visited IATs regularly, and it was the turn of 61+16 to represent MFG-3 at Nordholz in the SeaSearch line. As with many Atlantic operators, those of the Marineflieger have recently been updated with a new Texas Instruments radar, Loral ESM equipment and improved sonar. GB

The Airtech CN235MPA Persuader of the Irish Air Corps' Maritime Squadron based at Baldonnel arrived on Friday afternoon, marking Eire's first IAT showing. This maritime patrol variant is equipped with an APS-504 surveillance radar and FLIR, and was only delivered to the Air Corps two years ago. Confirmation of its appearance arrived late, as 252 is one of only two Persuaders in service with the small air arm, and the other was unserviceable until the end of the week. PRM

For the first time since 1993, the Israeli Air Force was represented at Fairford, by a KC-130H Hercules from 103 Squadron. Based at Lod, this is one of two such variants in service in Israel, and has a secondary maritime role which was illustrated by the airborne lifeboat displayed alongside it. The crew of this Hercules took home with them the Evans Halshaw Trophy for a Special Mention in the SeaSearch *Concours d'Elegance*. Brian J Atkinson/APM

One of the two Br1150 Atlantics in the SeaSearch line was this Italian aircraft (MM40123/30-10) from 30 Stormo/86 Gruppo at Cagliari. An upgrade programme, using various Atlantique ATL2 systems including the Thomson-CSF Iguane radar, has been in progress on the 18 aircraft operated by the Italians. PRM

Left: A welcome late addition to the SeaSearch meet was the Italian Air Force Agusta-Sikorsky AS-61R Pelican from 15 Stormo/83 Centro SAR, based at Rimini, with others within the wing (headquartered at Rome-Ciampino) being detached to Brindisi and Trapani. Equivalent to the USAF's HH-3F, the AMI operates over 30 licence-built Pelicans for combat rescue. They have recently been through an upgrade programme, adding improved defensive capabilities. PRM

The Royal Malaysian Air Force's contribution to the SeaSearch meet never actually made it over to the south side static park. C-130H-MP Hercules M30-07 from 4 Squadron at Subang (Kuala Lumpur) Airport, flew into a severe hailstorm over the Alps en route to Fairford that caused damage to the aircraft's nose. This is one of three MP versions used by the Malaysians for maritime patrol duties but with an airlift capability. In spite of the aircraft's problems, its crew received the Dowty Trophy in the SeaSearch competitions as they had travelled the greatest distance to attend. Here they are seen looking very proud in front of their damaged radome, receiving their award on the Saturday before flying out on the following day in order for the damaged C-130 to be repaired. JD/APM

The SeaSearch helicopter static displays included this colourful Agusta-Bell AB412SP from the Royal Netherlands Air Force's SAR Vlucht at Leeuwarden. It transitted through RAF Coltishall on its flights to and from Fairford. DJM

It has been several years since the Royal Norwegian Air Force provided a P-3 Orion at IAT, but the SeaSearch meet attracted this P-3N from 333 Skvadron at Andoya. Two such versions are used for, amongst other duties, training and fishery protection, alongside four newer P-3Cs which undertake the MR role. PRM

The Portuguese Air Force's contribution to SeaSearch came, as in 1989, in the form of an SA330C Puma from 751 Esquadra. This example and six others are flown from Montijo for Search and Rescue tasks. APM/JD

# SEASEARCH 96

It was an impressive illustration of present East-West relations, that this year's SeaSearch gathering included an Ilyushin Il-38 *May* from the Russian Navy making probably the type's first ground appearance at a NATO airfield. This aircraft, red 22, came from the Training Regiment at Ostrov. With about 40 in service, more Il-38s are used for ASW duties by Russia than any other type, the aircraft at Ostrov being used to instruct crews destined for operational *May* and Tu-142 *Bear* regiments. The badge shown is that of the Russian Northern Fleet. APM

The second visit of the South African Air Force to IAT was every bit as successful as the first. This C-130B Hercules from 28 Squadron, based at Waterkloof in Pretoria, carried the colourful markings applied to celebrate the South African Air Force's 75th anniversary last year. It carried home the Page Aerospace Trophy as Overall Winner of the SeaSearch *Concours d'Elegance*, following in the footsteps of the South African Boeing 707 that won the same accolade in the SkyTanker awards last year. SAAF C-130s are used in an SAR role, dropping dinghies and other equipment. PRM

Back in 1981, the Spanish sent a Fokker F-27-400MPA Friendship to appear at the first SeaSearch gathering. Fifteen years later, an example returned to IAT from 802 Escuadron based at Gando in the Canary Islands. The additional under-fuselage radome on this F-27 houses an APS-504 search radar, with a Bendix weather radar being carried in the nose. These Maritime Friendships are used, as the fuselage titling states, for various SAR duties. APM

SeaSearch 96 saw the IAT debut of the Swedish Air Force's AJSH37 Viggen, sent by F15 at Soderhamn. This aircraft is used in the all-weather over-water reconnaissance and anti-shipping strike roles. The special long-range camera pod and missiles were added to the aircraft for its static display. The SH37 fleet has joined AJ and SF variants in the AJS upgrade programme, which combines systems from all three original variants. The resulting designation of the converted aircraft and their final equipment fit alters depending on the version from which it was modified.
Mike Hadley

From the same unit as the Viggen, Soderhamn-based F15, came this equally rare and smart AS332M-1/Hkp10 Super Puma. The type has replaced Vertol 107s in the long-range search and rescue role.
BSS/APM

Illustrating its 'air ambulance' role in the SeaSearch static area was this Agusta-Bell AB412HP/Hkp11 from AF1 of the Swedish Army at Boden. BD/JD

There were two P-3C Orions from the US Navy on show, 158916/LL-30 came from VP-30 Pros based at NAS Jacksonville, FL (the main anti-submarine training unit) and 160612/LY belonging to VP-92 Minutemen from NAS South Weymouth, MA. As can be seen, unit markings (in some cases, quite colourful ones) are returning to the US Navy's P-3s. PRM/APM

Left: One of the two Hercules featured in the SeaSearch meet was this HC-130H(N) Combat Shadow variant. It is operated by the 102nd Rescue Squadron of the 106th RQW, based at Suffolk County Airport, NY as part of the New York Air National Guard. This relatively new aircraft lacks the characteristic Fulton recovery equipment and AN/ARD-17 aerial tracker in its radome of earlier HC-130s, but has improved avionics and communications equipment. The three HC-130H(N)s are used for refuelling USAF rescue helicopters and in an SAR role itself, having been transferred from the Alaska ANG. APM

Left: The 7th Special Operations Squadron, part of the 352nd SOG, flies five MC-130H Combat Talon II Hercules from its base at RAF Mildenhal, from which 87-0023 was brought to Fairford and featured in the SeaSearch line. DJM

Right: Now a regular visitor to IAT, the USAF Sikorsky HH-60G Pavehawk made the long journey from its base at NAS Keflavik, Iceland, where it is operated by the 85th Wing/56th RQS. This is a modified variant of the standard Blackhawk, used for combat rescue, and is equipped for long-range operations with an in-flight refuelling probe. GF

A pair of B-52H Stratofortresses came to Fairford from the 11th Bomb Squadron, part of the 2nd Bomb Wing at Barksdale AFB, LA. These formed part of the SeaSearch line, by virtue of the Squadron's secondary mine-laying role. In another maritime adaptation, B-52s can also carry the AGM-84 Harpoon anti-shipping missile. PRM

Oldest of the SeaSearch participants was C-47B Dakota 6 G-AMYJ, built in 1944 and one of seven veteran 'DC-3s' operated by Atlantic Air Transport from Coventry Airport as part of its Marine Pollution Control Unit (MPCU) contract with the Department of Transport. These aircraft have often been in the news for their work in assisting in the clean-ups of such as the *Braer* and *Sea Empress* oil spills. The MPCU has operational detachments at Manston and Inverness, its C-47s being equipped with spray bars which 'deliver' the dispersant with the help of an under-fuselage wind-driven pump. PRM

Left: G-TASK is one of two Cessna 404 Titans operated by Air Atlantique's MPCU. These twins provide fast-response reconnaissances of marine spills, using remote sensing equipment to survey the affected area. PRM

The Swedish Coastguard sent CASA C212 Aviocar SE-IVN/585 over as a colourful addition to the SeaSearch meet. Equipped with FLIR and other maritime surveillance equipment, this smart aircraft received a Special Mention in the Lockheed Martin Tactical Systems (UK) *Concours d'Elegance*. APM

Right: The third aircraft of Air Atlantique's SeaSearch contributions was BN-2A-26 Islander G-BCEN, that is flown by the company under contract to HM Coastguard. APM

Left: FR Aviation's Dornier 228-200 G-OMAF is operated on fishery patrol duties from RAF St Mawgan and its base at Bournemouth. There are three such specially-equipped Dornier 228s in service in this role with FRA. DJM

Right: The prize for the aircraft that travelled the shortest distance to attend SeaSearch (if there had been one) would have gone to the preserved ex-RAF Whirlwind HAR10 (XJ729). Owned by Austen Associates, this ex-No 22 Squadron SAR helicopter is based at Cricklade, just a few miles away from Fairford. PRM

Making only its second UK appearance, the Beriev A-40 Mermaid, 378, was sent to Fairford by the manufacturer at Taganrog, for whom this aircraft is a demonstrator. This, the largest amphibian in the world, has been designed for ASW/maritime reconnaissance guise as the Be-44, and an SAR version the Be-42, along with various transport variants. However, no firm orders have been placed by the Russian armed forces, as yet. APM

Nearly 30 of the world's air arms sent aircraft for the static displays at The Royal International Air Tattoo. These ranged from a debut by the Ukraine to return visits by the Russian Navy and the Royal Air Force of Oman.

**Right:** Least powerful of all the RAF types on show was Grob Vigilant T1 ZH191 from No 612 Volunteer Gliding School at the former RAF Abingdon, having moved there from Halton. This, the RAF variant of the G109B powered glider, entered service in early 1990 with the VGSs and with the Central Gliding School of the Air Cadets. GF

**Left:** A pair of Bulldog T1s, XX622/B and XX709/E, were provided for the static by the Yorkshire Universities Air Squadron. The YUAS now incorporates No 9 Air Experience Flight since the re-organisation of the RAF's basic training units, and moved earlier this year to RAF Linton-on-Ouse having initially been stationed at Church Fenton following Finningley's closure in 1995. APM

**Right:** A contribution from No 3 FTS at RAF Cranwell was this Dominie XS726/T. All of the 11 examples of the navigation trainer remaining in service are being updated by Thorn EMI and Marshall Aerospace, the programme involving installation of a Super Searcher maritime surveillance radar and other associated improvements. DJM

No 230 Squadron at RAF Aldergrove, Belfast, flies its Puma HC1s, such as XW234 which it sent for the IAT static display, to support the British Army in the Province. In a re-organisation of the RAF's Support Helicopter forces, No 72 Squadron (currently operating the Wessex) will re-equip with Pumas at the same base. PRM

Left: One of No 1 Squadron's Harrier GR7s, ZD322, was put in a 'hide' setting, complete with a comprehensive equipment display. PRM

Below: No 11 Squadron is one of two units currently operating the Tornado F3 from RAF Leeming, and provided two aircraft, ZE934/DX and the unmarked ZE201 for the static display. JD

Below: No 13 Squadron sent two Tornados for the static park, with GR1 ZG752 (carrying an 'XIII' tail-code in recognition of the unit's 80th anniversary last year) being accompanied from RAF Marham by GR1A ZG729/M. They were joined in the Tornado line-up of RAF and German Air Force aircraft (left) by GR1A ZG706/E, one of four that operate alongside the Air Warfare Centre's SAOEU Harriers at Boscombe Down. PRM/Ian Grainger

All three of the RAF tanker units from 'just up the road' at Brize Norton were represented in the static park, with TriStar KC1 ZD952 coming from No 216 Squadron.

Herman J Sixma

The conversion of No 10 Squadron's VC10 C1s to C1K tanker standard is now virtually complete. XV109, displaying the underwing Flight Refuelling Mk32 hose/drum units, made the short trip across from RAF Brize Norton for static display. JD

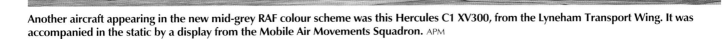

Another aircraft appearing in the new mid-grey RAF colour scheme was this Hercules C1 XV300, from the Lyneham Transport Wing. It was accompanied in the static by a display from the Mobile Air Movements Squadron. APM

Above: No 6 Squadron at RAF Coltishall provided Jaguar GR1A XZ385 for the static park. The Norfolk station also houses Nos 41 and 54 Squadrons, all three units currently pooling their aircraft. DJM

Right: Hawk T1As XX195/CA and XX247/CM came in from RAF Leeming, where they are operated by No 100 Squadron. The unit's fleet moved to its current home from Finningley in September of last year. These Hawks operate as the Joint Forward Air Control Standards & Trials Unit (JFACSTU) having been part of the now-disbanded No 6 FTS. Its new fin badge, seen on the black-painted aircraft, includes an anchor, eagle and machine gun, illustrating JFACSTU's involvement with all three services. APM

Above: Another veteran Wessex HC2 in the static display was XR505/WA, named *Aries*, from No 2 FTS. It is based at RAF Shawbury, where the new tri-service Defence Helicopter Flying Training School will form in 1997. JD

No 7 Squadron at RAF Odiham sent Chinook HC2 ZH777/NY to Fairford, one of the unit's 17 examples of this heavy-lift helicopter in service. All of the original HC1 fleet has now been updated by Boeing Helicopters to CH-47D standard, with 14 new-build HC2 (of which this was one) and HC3 aircraft currently being delivered. PRM

# ROYAL NAVY

This year saw the first appearance of RN Sea Harrier FA2s at Fairford. Operated by No 800 NAS at Yeovilton, ZD607/123 appeared in the Harrier 30th anniversary static line. PRM

# ARMY AIR CORPS

There were two Army Air Corps helicopters from Middle Wallop in the static park, with *Blue Eagles*' spare Gazelle AH1 of No 670 Squadron( (right) joined by a No 671 Squadron Lynx AH7 (above). APM

Top: The ETPS operates two Jaguar T2s, with XX145 appearing in the colourful 'raspberry ripple' section of the IAT static display. PRM

Above: A particularly heavily-utilised member of the ETPS fleet is early Lynx 7 ZD560 which joined its Gazelle counterpart on static display. APM

Below: The only two Canberras remaining in the hands of the MoD(PE) trials establishments are with the DTEO at Llanbedr. The target-tug Canberra B(TT)2 WK128 was the only military-operated example of the type at IAT. PRM

Top left: Flown in from Boscombe Down was the ETPS Gazelle HT2 XZ936, one of the fleet's rotary-wing 'classrooms'. APM

Above: A regular visitor to IAT is the unique Hawk T1 ASTRA, XX341 from the ETPS. Like the Basset, it illustrates a variety of aircraft handling qualities, albeit at higher speeds, and has recently been used on fly-by-wire system trials. PRM

Left There were two Hunters from Boscombe Down in the static park. Hunter T7 XL564 is one of a pair of two-seaters flying with the ETPS, while FGA9 XE601 (illustrated) comes from the DTEO's Fixed Wing Test Squadron. The FGA9 was flown in to Fairford by Sqn Ldr Dave Southwood, who gave a spirited arrival display including a demonstration of the aircraft's special underwing NBC warfare simulation tanks. PRM

There was a welcome static appearance from the Empire Test Pilots School's Beagle Basset CC1 the second military production example of the type. It remains in use at Boscombe Down as a 'flying classroom', able to illustrate different aircraft handling characteristics using its Variable Stability System. BD

# MINISTRY OF DEFENCE (PE)

This aerial view shows part of the colourful line-up of MoD test and evaluation aircraft, including the only Harvard IIB left in service with the DTEO at Boscombe Down. KF183 is used as a slow-speed photo ship and for tailwheel conversion and continuation training. PRM

# CANADIAN ARMED FORCES
## (Forces Armées Canadienne)

The Royal IAT saw the first UK display appearance by an Airbus CC-150 Polaris from the Canadian Armed Forces. No 437 Squadron, attached to 8 Wing at CFB Trenton, operates five of these ex-Canadian Airlines aircraft in the transport role, one of them fitted with a VIP interior. This particular example had recently been involved in UN support duties, and carried a small badge in recognition. APM/PRM

**Left:** The Czechs only operate one Mil Mi-24DU, the unarmed trainer variant of the basic *Hind-D*, so it was particularly welcome at Fairford this year, in support of the three-ship Mi-24 display team. It is based with them under 331.vrtl at Prerov. Apart from having a faired-over nose turret, this version is also equipped with full dual controls. It arrived in company with the three display aircraft and an escorting AAC Gazelle from Middle Wallop. BD

The colourful Czech Air Force Let L-410UVP-E9 Turbolet (below right) in the static came from 61.dlt, part of 6.zDL at Prague-Kbely. This is the air force's main transport wing, operating a variety of different variants of this sturdy light transport. Also from 61.dlt came the UK show debut of the Antonov An-24RV (right), with 5803 being one of four such aircraft in service alongside the L-410s at Kbely in the passenger and VIP transport roles. PRM/APM

Supporting the two-seat Czech Air Force MiG-21 in the flying display was this single-seat MiG-21MF *Fishbed* 7711, like its airborne counterpart operated by the LZO at Line. This example visited IAT two years ago, and still carries the distinctive colours of the DFIII Acrobatic Group, that was first formed with MiG-15s in 1957.

John Chase

# ROYAL DANISH AIR FORCE
## (Kongelige Danske Flyvevaaban)

**Above** The Royal Danish Air Force has provided its combat aircraft at many Tattoos over the years, and 1996 was no exception. Eskadrilles 723 and 726 at Aalborg sent F-16A and F-16B Fighting Falcons E-607 and ET-199 for static display. PRM

**Left:** The Royal Danish Air Force's SAAB T-17 Supporters, such as T-409 and T-426 this year, have visited many IATs. These two came from the Flyveskolan (FLSK) at Avno, where they are used as basic trainers, but the type is also flown by the Base Flights at front-line stations and the Danish Army. APM

# ROYAL DANISH ARMY
## (Haerens Flyvetjaeneste)

There were four Royal Danish Army SA550C-2 Fennecs in the static park, that made formation flypasts on arrival and departure. Based at Vandel, the Fennec fleet is operated by the Panservaerns-Helikopter Kompagni (Anti-Tank Helicopter Platoon). In Danish service, they are fitted with four Hughes TOW BGM-71 anti-tank missiles, augmented by the SAAB/Emerson Heli-TOW system. PRM

## (L'Aviation Legère de l'Armée de Terre)

There were two different French Army Pumas in the IAT static park this year. The older SA330B Puma, 1036/ARB (below), came from EHM-2 of 4 RHCM at Phalsbourg, with the AS532UL Cougar/Super Puma, 2325/AIA (above) belonging to EHM-3 with the same Regiment. DJM/APM

# FRENCH ARMY LIGHT AVIATION
## (L'Aviation Legère de l'Armée de Terre)

The French Army Light Aviation contingent included two fixed-wing types from 3 GHL at Rennes. The now familiar Cessna F406 Caravan II (right) was this time 0008/ABM (both examples used by the service have been repainted in this smart white livery), and it was joined by one of the liaison unit's two SOCATA TBM700s (below). This was the UK show debut of an in-service example of this single-engined turboprop light transport. DJM

Smallest of the French Army helicopter types on show was this SA342L1 Gazelle, 4211/CYU from EHAP-2 of 1 RHC at Phalsbourg. 18 examples of the 'L' variant are flown by ALAT, having originally been destined for Chinese service but then transferred back to France before delivery. JD

Left: The special markings carried on the forward fuselage of Transall C-160D 50+52 from LTG-62 at Holzdorf indicate the type's 300,000 flying hours now notched up with the unit, and this Lufttransportgeschwader's own 15th anniversary. A major refurbishment programme should see the German Transall fleet remaining in service until at least 2010. PRM

Right: The Luftwaffe now operates far fewer Alpha Jets than previously, as more of its flying training has been transferred to the USA. However, the Fluglehrgruppe at Furstenfeldbruck (FLG FFB) has retained over 30 examples, such as 41+56 seen here, for lead-in combat training. It is planned that the unit will disband in 1997. PRM

Right: Another front-line German fast jet type represented in the static display was the Tornado IDS, with 46+04 coming from JBG-38 at Jever. DJM

Left: Although it was sadly withdrawn from the flying display, the Luftwaffe's MiG-29A 29+11 from JG-73 was a welcome sight on the ground. Inherited from the East German Air Force after re-unification, these Fulcrums are now operated by 731 Staffel at Laage, in the former DDR. Chris Schenk

# GERMAN ARMY AVIATION
## (Heeresflieger)

Three MBB BO105Ps were contributed by HFR-26, based at Buckeburg. This version, designated PAH-1 (Panzerabwehrhubschrauber – Anti-tank helicopter) in the anti-tank role, using Euromissile HOT weapons, will eventually be replaced by the Eurocopter Tiger. PRM

Representing the German Army's Sikorsky CH-53G fleet was 84+87 from HFR-15 at Rheine-Bentlage. Three medium-transport helicopter regiments are equipped with the type, the others being stationed at Mendig and Laupheim. PRM

# GERMAN NAVY
## (Marineflieger)

As well as putting one of its Tornados through its paces in the flying display, the German Navy contributed Tornado IDS 45+53 from MFG-2 at Eggebek for the static display, seen here shortly after arrival at Fairford. APM

# ITALIAN AIR FORCE
## (Aeronautica Militare Italiano)

A regular highlight of the IAT static park is the appearance of Italian Air Force F-104S/ASA Starfighters. This year was no exception with two aircraft coming from 5 Stormo/23 Gruppo at Cervia-San Giorgo, one of which was painted in the IAF's new air defence grey livery. The now-completed ASA modifications, adding improved radar and weaponry and new avionics, should see these F-104s through until replacement by EF2000. Steve Screech/DJM

# ROYAL JORDANIAN AIR FORCE
## (Al Quwwat Al-Jawwiya Al-Malakiya Al Urduniya)

No 3 Squadron, the *Guts Airline* of the Royal Jordanian Air Force based at Amman-King Abdullah Airport, has provided a C-130H Hercules for the IAT static for many years now. This year, it was 347 on display, and once again it brought with it an extensive exhibition on Jordan and its air arm, which was well-attended over the weekend. DJM

The three new Royal Netherlands Air Force transports from 334 Squadron at Eindhoven, all UK airshow debutants, were among the stars of the static displays. Smallest of the gleaming trio was a Fokker 60U (above), the type that is replacing the F-27M. The F-60Us are equipped with better defensive systems including chaff/flare dispensers and ALR-69 RWRs. They are faster and having a bigger load-carrying capacity, thanks to the large cargo door, an F-16's complete F100 engine can be carried without the need for dismantling. PRM

The appearance of McDonnell Douglas KDC-10, T-264 Prins Bernhard, completed an impressive trio from 334 Squadron. This and the other example in KLu service are ex-Martinair DC-10s, converted at Amsterdam-Schipol to tanker-cargo/passenger transport configuration. Both carry a unique new remote-controlled boom operation system, with the operator himself sited immediately behind the cockpit and steering the boom via television displays. PRM

MBB BO105CB B-68 from 299 Squadron, Gilze Rijen, which has now become an all-helicopter base as the KLu receives new rotary-wing types. In the first half of the next decade, all of the Bolkows will be replaced. PRM

The Royal IAT welcomed the largest Royal Netherlands Air Force contingent ever seen at a British airshow, which naturally included a large collection of F-16s. From Volkel, 306 Squadron sent F-16A(R) J-633, this unit's single-seaters all being reconaissance versions, and 311 Squadron sent F-16B J-066. Nos 322 and 323 Squadrons at Leeuwarden provided a further pair of two-seaters, J-209 and J-655 respectively. Re-organisation of the Dutch F-16 fleet has left three units at Volkel, two at Leeuwarden and two more at Twenthe, and all the Squadrons are to receive mid-life update aircraft by 2002. BD

The Royal Netherlands Air Force 334 Squadron also operates two C-130H-30 Hercules, with G-273, named *Ben Swagerman* (the first to enter service) appearing at Fairford. Delivered in 1994, the two Hercules represented the first major additions to the Dutch airlift capability, which has of course since grown even more considerably. As the small blue badge carried on its fuselage testifies, G-273 was detached to Rimini in Italy in support of IFOR operations in Bosnia. Both the C-130s have also seen much use in Africa. BD

# NATO
## (North Atlantic Treaty Organisation)

Boeing E-3A LX-N90449 is one of 14 AWACS platforms operated by the NATO AEW Force from Geilenkirchen. The E-3A Component sadly suffered its first casualty in the week leading up to the show, when one of the aircraft was lost, thankfully without any major harm to the crew, at the Forward Operating Base at Preveza in Greece. It ran off the runway into the sea on landing. PRM

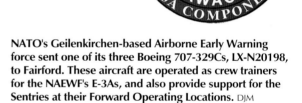

NATO's Geilenkirchen-based Airborne Early Warning force sent one of its three Boeing 707-329Cs, LX-N20198, to Fairford. These aircraft are operated as crew trainers for the NAEWF's E-3As, and also provide support for the Sentries at their Forward Operating Locations. DJM

# ROYAL NORWEGIAN AIR FORCE
## (Kongelige Norske Luftforsvaret)

F-5B Freedom Fighters 136 and 243 are among the 23-strong fleet of these and single-seat F-5As operated by 336 Skvadron at Rygge, as lead-in fighter trainers. Sierra Industries is implementing the Tiger-PAWS update on 15 of the aircraft, providing them with improved avionics and weapons systems. Norwegian F-5s have long been IAT visitors, including a pair at the first show at North Weald 25 years ago. DJM

# ROYAL AIR FORCE OF OMAN

## (At Quwwat al Jawwiya al Sultanat Oman)

No 4 Squadron at Seeb now operates the Royal Air Force of Oman's three C-130H Hercules. DJM

# RUSSIAN AIR FORCE

## (Voenno-Vozdushniye Sily Rossioki Federatsii)

Supporting the Beriev A-40 and attracting much attention in the static park with its unusual lines, was Antonov An-72A *Coaler* RA-72972. Although it carries Aeroflot's colours and titling, this is a military aircraft, serving with VVS Transport Aviation of the Russian Air Force. A large proportion of the Air Force's airlift fleet still carries Aeroflot liveries.
PRM/APM

# SLOVAK AIR FORCE
## (Slovacke Vojenske Letectvo)

All the Slovak Air Force's two-seat MiG-29UBs, are painted in this distinctive tiger-striped livery. It is one of three trainers now in service with 1 Letka of 31 SLK based at Sliac, after the delivery of a third aircraft from Russia in 1995. BD

Support for the Slovak MiGs came from the air arm's Antonov An-12BP of 1 Letka/32 ZmDK, the transport wing based at Piestany. GF/PRM

One of Ala 35's Airtech CN235M-100s, T19B-12/35-30 operated by 352 Escuadron from Getafe, represented the Spanish Air Force transport fleet.
PRM

Another welcome Spanish Air Force static item was an RF-4C Phantom from 123 Escuadron of Ala 12 at Torrejon. These ex-USAF reconnaissance aircraft have been equipped with APQ-172 terrain-following radar, new ECM equipment and other modifications.
DJM/BD/JD

# SWEDISH AIR FORCE
## (Svenska Flygvapnet)

The C-130E/Tp84 Hercules from F7 Satenas that came in support of the Viggen and Team 60 is the oldest Hercules in service with a European air arm. APM

# SWEDISH ARMY AIR CORPS
## (Svenska Armeflygkar)

The Swedish Army's MBB BO105CB/Hkp9 in the static came from AF1. These aircraft are HeliTOW-equipped in the anti-tank role. APM

**Above:** A second Ukrainian Air Force Su-27A *Flanker*, 48, from 831 IAP at Mirgorod, was surrounded by onlookers in the static line, who were able to talk to its crew and climb into its cockpit. This aircraft carried the same special national markings as that in the flying programme. PRM/APM

**Right:** As part of the Ukrainian Air Force's UK debut, this Ilyushin Il-76MD *Candid*, UR-78820, attended in support of the two Su-27s. The air arm's Il-76s are augmented in the heavy transport role by An-12s, both types serving with 243 OSAP (Independent Mixed Aviation Regiment) at Lvov, part of the 14 VA (Air Army). PRM

Right: Largest aircraft on show was the USAF Air Mobility Command's C-5B Galaxy, from the 436th Airlift Wing's 3rd AS at Dover AFB, DE. It was a popular walk-through exhibit. PRM

Below: Neither of the C-141B Starlifters present this year came from a 'regular' USAF unit. 65-0245 is flown by the 730th AS, Air Force Reserve while 67-0029, came from the 155th AS based at Memphis International Airport as part of the Tennessee ANG. The latter's callsign, appropriately enough, was Elvis 11. PRM

Below: There were two C-21A Learjets in the Fairford static park. 84-0085 came from the 86th Airlift Wing's 76th AS at Ramstein, and 84-0068 is operated by the 7005th Air Base Squadron, HQ US European Command at Stuttgart International Airport. Both are used as high-speed passenger/VIP transports. PRM

Flown from and to Mildenhall before and after its IAT appearance, RC-135U 64-14847/OF is normally based at Offutt AFB, NE with the 55th Wing's 38th Reconnaissance Squadron. The 95th RS handles the Temporary Duty (TDY) carried out by these and other 'RC' variants at Mildenhall, from where they have regularly flown on surveillance missions over the former Yugoslavia. APM

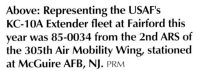

**Above:** Representing the USAF's KC-10A Extender fleet at Fairford this year was 85-0034 from the 2nd ARS of the 305th Air Mobility Wing, stationed at McGuire AFB, NJ. PRM

**Right:** As usual at Fairford there were several KC-135s present. One of the three Air National Guard aircraft in the static display was 60-0367, sent by the 121st ARW/166th ARS of the Ohio ANG. The *Wabash Cannonball* nose-art belongs to KC-135R 63-8023 of the 100th ARW/351st ARS at RAF Mildenhall, USAFE's only permanently-based Stratotanker unit. PRM/BD

**Right:** The 28th BW/37th BS' second B-1B Lancer flown in on the Friday was 86-0111 *Dakota Lightning* from Elsworth AFB. BD

**Below:** A McDonnell Douglas C-17A Globemaster III from Air Mobility Command made its first visit to IAT this year. The 17th Airlift Squadron, attached to the 437th AW at Charleston AFB, SC, sent 94-0067 to Fairford for what should be the first of many appearances at the show by this new transport. PRM

The two USAFE F-15 Eagles at IAT this year were both F-15Cs, 86-0167/LN and 86-0175/LN, based at RAF Lakenheath with the 493rd FS/48th FW. These interceptors have been stationed at the Suffolk base alongside the Wing's F-15Es since 1994. DJM

Two USAFE Fighter Wings provided F-16s at the Tattoo. The 31st FW at Aviano in Italy sent a pair of F-16Cs, 88-0526/AV and 89-2039/AV, both from the 555th FS, known as *Triple Nickel*. F-16C 92-3918/SP and two-seat F-16D 91-0474/SP are on the strength of the 23rd FS, part of the 52nd FW – the Wild Weasel unit at Spangdahlem, Germany. BD

The only A-10A Thunderbolt IIs now in service with United States Air Forces Europe (USAFE) are flown by the 81st Fighter Squadron/ 52nd FW at Spangdahlem in the Eifel region of Germany. JD

Right: One of the many USAF Hercules on show was C-130H 90-1792/OH, provided by the 164th Airlift Squadron of the 179th AW. The unit is based at Mansfield Lahm Airport, and forms part of the Ohio Air National Guard. An even newer example, however, was 93-7312/CR, named *Spirit of Summit 38* from the 731st AS, an Air Force Reserve squadron from Peterson AFB, CO that reports to the 302nd AW. PRM

Left: A contributor to IAT since the early Tattoos, the 193rd Special Operations Squadron, Pennsylvania Air National Guard sent EC-130E Hercules 63-7828 from its base at Harrisburg IAP to Fairford this year. The unit's four Rivet Rider variants, of which this is one, are tasked with COMINT (communications intelligence) and SIGINT (signals intelligence) missions, sending TV and radio programmes in times of war or natural disasters and, as in the Gulf, for psychological warfare purposes. This particular EC-130 has recently been through an upgrade programme, allowing better colour TV broadcasting following an earlier modification. GF

Below: Another 'first' at IAT this year was the debut appearance at any UK airshow of an AC-130U Hercules 'gunship' from the USAF's Special Operations Command. 90-0166, appropriately named *Hellraiser*, came from the 4th Special Operations Squadron of the 16th SOW, based at Hurlburt Field, Florida. PRM

Above: The new version's armament consists of a single L-60 Bofors 40mm cannon and a 105mm M102 howitzer, plus a 25mm GAU-12 cannon with 3000 rounds. This latest version on the Spectre gunship theme uses new targeting equipment, unrivalled in its accuracy - a Hughes AN/APQ-180 fire control radar, AAQ-117 FLIR, ALQ-172 jammer and low-light TV are among the systems fitted in the 13 new-build aircraft, being converted from C-130H production line standard by Rockwell. PRM

A late arrival for the static park was AH-64A Apache 86-8950 from the US Army's 6-6th Cavalry Regiment based at Illesheim in Germany. The European-based US Army units are not scheduled to receive new AH-64Ds until early in the next century. PRM

# UNITED STATES MARINE CORPS

Two US Marine Corps KC-130s were lined up in the heavy aircraft static park – the KC-130F 149803/GR, came from the tanker/transport training unit VMGRT-253 at Cherry Point MCAS, NC, and a later KC-130R, 160015/QB was from VMGR-352 based at El Toro, CA.
BSS

Another familiar sight at IAT is a Beech UC-12M Super King Air from the US Naval Air Facility at RAF Mildenhall, with 163840/8G coming this year. The NAFs use these small twin-turboprops for liaison and communications duties. GF

# CIVILIANS

The Micro Aviation B22S Bantam ZK-TII is a new microlight design from New Zealand, which is being marketed from Scotland by Aviation Quality Services. It was displayed on the company's stand over the weekend, attracting a good deal of public interest. PRM

Right: A late arrival on Friday for the static display after technical problems at its home base was Canberra TT18 WJ680 (G-BURM), the first example of the classic multi-role twin-jet to have been put onto the UK civil register three years ago. Now housed at North Weald, Charlie-Tango is owned by Mitchell Aircraft Ltd and retains its former RAF No 100 Squadron markings worn during its final service days at Wyton. PRM

Right: In IAT's Silver Jubilee year, it was very appropriate that Fairford should again be visited by Bruno Stocker from Switzerland in his Cessna 340A HB-LPK. Bruno is the Tattoo's most regular visiting pilot, first in the 1970s when he brought the leader and other members of the *Patrouille Suisse* over before the team ever appeared itself. He has continued to visit in the Cessna almost every year (a rare exception being 1995). BD

The appropriately registered Cherokee 140 G-FIAT is owned by the Royal Air Force Benevolent Fund. It is used for continuation flying by disabled pilots who have completed their Flying Scholarships awarded by the Fund in memory of Sir Douglas Bader. The aircraft can be fitted with special hand controls for this purpose. APM

Above: New with the Dutch Dakota Association this year is this Douglas DC-4, ZS-NUR/PH-DDS. It was previously flown by the South African Air Force and South African Airways, before being sold to the DDA who base it at Amsterdam-Schipol. This is the only DC-4 currently operated in Europe. PRM

A pair of Shorts 360-100s brought more 'fly-in' visitors to Fairford. G-ZAPG was from Stansted-based Titan Airways, with G-OJSY being on the fleet of BAC Express. DJM

Left: One of the newer types in Atlantic Airways' inventory is SA227AC Metro III, G-BUKA. A marked contrast compared with the veteran DC-3s that make up the majority of the fleet. DJM

Below: Two different Dakotas, still in commercial service in the UK, brought charter passengers into Fairford. The familiar G-AMPZ, a C-47B, is operated by Air Atlantique from Coventry Airport, while C-47A G-DAKK is new on the scene this year, being operated by South Coast Airways from its base at Bournemouth. BD

# VISITING & SUPPORT AIRCRAFT

As usual, there were two light transports of the Swiss Air Force's Dubendorf-based VIP Flight present to support the Patrouille Suisse and bring in VIPs, but this year only one Learjet 35A, T-781. Its sister aircraft T-782 has now been sold, and instead the second Swiss support aircraft was Beech Super King Air 350 HB-GII. PRM/APM

Below: The Empire Test Pilots School's BAC 1-11/479FU ZE432 acted as a ferry for the crews of the other aircraft from Boscombe Down, and as such appeared on Friday and Monday. PRM

Below: No less than four Transall C-160Ds from the Turkish Air Force visited Fairford in support of the Turkish Stars. Two flew in and out again on the Wednesday, with two more doing the same on the following Monday, all operated by 221 Filo of 12 Hava Ulastirma Ana US at Erkilet. APM

# VISITING & SUPPORT AIRCRAFT

Right: A party of RAF VIPs arrived in BAe 146 CC2 ZE702. This is one of three such aircraft operated by No 32 (The Royal) Squadron, based at RAF Northolt. PRM

Left: A familiar visitor to IAT is a German Air Force Let L-410UVP-E Turbolet. Present this year was 53+11, from Flugbereitschaftstaffel 3 based at Berlin-Tegel, bringing in Luftwaffe General Mende and his wife. PRM

Below: This was the last time that a Royal Netherlands Air Force Fokker F-27-100 Friendship will visit IAT, as the three remaining VIP transport variants are being phased out in favour of Fokker 60s. C-2 from No 334 Squadron at Eindhoven stayed for the whole IAT weekend. APM

Originally scheduled to be a static participant, the DH84 Dragon EI-ABI named Iolar, owned by the Irish national airline Aer Lingus, arrived on Saturday and departed the following morning. This example (originally G-AECZ) is 60 years old this year, and is painted to represent the carrier's first ever aircraft. Mark Tuffin

Right: Another VIP transport to visit was Tp102 Gulfstream IV 102001/021 from the Swedish Air Force. It is operated by F16 at Uppsala, this being the only such transport-configured example serving with the Flygvapnet. DJM

Right: Regular sights at Tattoos over the years have been Citation II G-BFRM and PA-23 Aztec 250E G-BATN, operated as transports by Marshall Aerospace from its base at Cambridge Airport. BD

One of two Sikorsky S-76s operating into Fairford during the airshow weekend, S-76-II Plus G-BJGX is owned by Bristow Helicopters and flew in a number of VIPs for the Sunday display. BSS

# EMERGENCY SERVICES

In keeping with all airshows, The Royal International Air Tattoo has to have an emergency services organisation that can respond effectively to any incident in the air or on the ground. It also has to provide the necessary services to care for the large numbers of people – spectators and volunteers – assembled at Fairford. This requires comprehensive medical, fire-fighting, police and incident facilities on the airfield and a detailed action plan involving local and national services in the area. In the weeks before the Air Tattoo, plans are laid, meetings are held and routines practiced, culminating in a major accident exercise at Fairford on the Thursday before the airshow. Although all of the services were called into action during the weekend, none of the aviation-related incidents were serious – a Harrier suffered a bird strike, the Vimy landed on one engine, and a Phantom and Tornado had hot brakes.

**Above: A Jet Provost composite airframe from RAF Halton's fire section was used, with a number of wrecked cars to add realism to the practice crash.** APM/BSS

**Above: Fire crews on stand-by after the TTTE Tornado had 'smoking' brakes when it taxied in.** BSS

**Right: A Wessex HC2 from No 60 Squadron was on hand to assist the emergency services during the show.** APM

**Below: Emergency helicopter medical services were provided by this MBB Bo 105 from Police Aviation Services at Gloucester.** BSS

**An impressive parade of fire appliances and ambulances preceded the flying display on both days.** PRM

## PARTICIPANTS AT THE ROYAL INTERNATIONAL AIR TATTOO
## RAF FAIRFORD 20 & 21 JULY 1996

### AIRCRAFT IN THE STATIC DISPLAYS (SOUTH SIDE OF AIRFIELD)

| | | |
|---|---|---|
| BAe 125 CC3 | ZD621 | 32(The Royal) Sqn |
| Bulldog T1 | XX622/B | Yorkshire UAS |
| | XX709/E | Yorkshire UAS |
| Chinook HC2 | ZH777/NY | 27(R) Sqn |
| Dominie T1 | XS726/T | 3 FTS |
| Harrier GR7 | ZD322/03 | 1 Sqn |
| | ZG472/O | AWC/SAOEU |
| Harrier T10 | ZH662/R | HOCU/20(R) Sqn |
| Hawk T1 | XX236/PK | 4 FTS/19(R) Sqn |
| Hawk T1A | XX195/CA | 100 Sqn |
| | XX247/CM | 100 Sqn |
| Hercules C1 | XV300 | LTW |
| Jaguar GR1A | XZ385 | 6 Sqn |
| Jaguar GR1A (replica) | XZ363/A | EP&TU |
| Jetstream T1 | XX493/L | 3 FTS/45(R) Sqn |
| Nimrod MR2 | XV231 | 206 Sqn/Kinloss Wing |
| | XV232 | 201 Sqn/Kinloss Wing |
| Puma HC1 | XW234 | 230 Sqn |
| Tornado F3 | ZG795/CB | 5 Sqn |
| | ZE201 | 11 Sqn |
| | ZE934/DX | 11 Sqn |
| | ZE735/AL | F3 OCU/56(R) Sqn |
| | ZE794/HQ | 111 Sqn |
| Tornado GR1 | ZG752/XIII | 13 Sqn |
| Tornado GR1A | ZG729/M | 13 Sqn |
| | ZG706/E | AWC/SAOEU |
| Tornado GR1 (replica) | ZA368/AJ-P | EP&TU |
| Tristar KC1 | ZD952 | 216 Sqn |
| Tucano T1 | ZF162 | 1 FTS |
| VC10 C1K | XV109 | 10 Sqn |
| VC10 K2 | ZA143/D | 101 Sqn |
| Vigilant T1 | ZH191 | 612 VGS |
| Wessex HC2 | XR505/WA Aries | 2 FTS |
| | XV724 | SARTU |

### Royal Navy

| | | |
|---|---|---|
| Lynx HAS3S | XZ698/303 | 815 NAS |
| Sea Harrier FA2 | ZD607/123 | 800 NAS |
| Sea King HAR5 | ZA167/CU-825 | 771 NAS |
| Sea King HAS6 | XV665/505 | 810 NAS |
| Sea King HC4 | ZD480/E | 845 NAS IFOR |

### Army Air Corps

| | | |
|---|---|---|
| Gazelle AH1 | XX405/C1 | 670 Sqn Blue Eagles |
| Lynx AH7 | XZ193/I | 671 Sqn |

### Ministry of Defence (Procurement Executive)

| | | |
|---|---|---|
| Basset CC1 | XS743 | ETPS |
| Canberra B(TT)2 | WK128 | DTEO Llanbedr |
| Eurofighter 2000 (replica) | – | BAe |
| Gazelle HT2 | XZ936 | ETPS |
| Harvard IIB | KF183 | DTEO A&EC/FWTS |
| Hawk T1 ASTRA | XX341 | ETPS |
| Hawk 200 (replica) | – | BAe |
| Hunter FGA9 | XE601 | DTEO A&EC/FWTS |
| Hunter T7 | XL564 | ETPS |
| Jaguar T2 | XX145 | ETPS |
| JAS39 Gripen (replica) | – | BAe |
| Lynx 7 | ZD560 | ETPS |

### Brazilian Air Force

| | | |
|---|---|---|
| C-130H Hercules | 2465 | 1 GTT/2 Esq |

### Canadian Armed Forces

| | | |
|---|---|---|
| CC-150 Polaris | 15005/204 | 437 Sqn/8 Wg |
| | | [UN markings] |
| CP-140 Aurora | 140113 | 405 Sqn/14 Wg |

### Czech Air Force

| | | |
|---|---|---|
| Antonov An-24RV Coke | 5803 | 61.dlt/6.zDL |
| Let L-410UVP-E9 Turbolet | 2601 | 61.dlt/6.zDL |
| MiG-21MF Fishbed | 7711 | LZO |
| Mil Mi-24DU Hind | 6050 (7306050) | 331.vrlt/33.zVL |

### Royal Danish Air Force

| | | |
|---|---|---|
| F-16A Fighting Falcon | E-607 | Esk 723 |
| F-16B Fighting Falcon | ET-199 | Esk 726 |
| Gulfstream III | F-313 | Esk 721 |
| SAAB T-17 Supporter | T-409 | FLSK |
| | T-426 | FLSK |
| Sikorsky S-61A | U-275 | Esk 722 |

### Royal Danish Army

| | | |
|---|---|---|
| SA550C-2 Fennec | P-276 | P-HK |
| | P-275 | P-HK |
| | P-369 | P-HK |
| | P-319 | P-HK |

### Royal Danish Navy

| | | |
|---|---|---|
| Lynx Mk90 | S-256 | Esk 722 |

### French Army Light Aviation

| | | |
|---|---|---|
| AS532UL Cougar/ | | |
| Super Puma | 2325/AIA | 4 RHCM/EHM-3 |
| Cessna F406 Caravan II | 0008/ABM | 3 GHL |
| SA330B Puma | 1036/ARB | 4 RHCM/EHM-2 |
| SA342 Gazelle | 4211/CYU | 1 RHC/EHAP-2 |
| SOCATA TBM700 | 100/ABP | 3 GHL |

### French Navy

| | | |
|---|---|---|
| Falcon 10(MER) | 143 | 57S |
| SA321G Super Frelon | 162 | 32F |

### German Air Force

| | | |
|---|---|---|
| Alpha Jet A | 41+56 | FLG FFB |
| F-4F Phantom II | 38+04 | JG-71 |
| MiG-29A Fulcrum | 29+11 (25128) | JG-73 |
| Tornado IDS | 46+04 | JBG-38 |
| Transall C-160D | 50+52 | LTG-62 |

### German Army

| | | |
|---|---|---|
| MBB BO105P | 87+00 | HFR-26 |
| | 87+98 | HFR-26 |
| | 87+02 | HFR-26 |
| Sikorsky CH-53G | 84+87 | HFR-15 |

### German Navy

| | | |
|---|---|---|
| Br1150 Atlantic | 61+16 | MFG-3 |
| Sea King Mk41 | 89+66 | MFG-5 |
| Tornado IDS | 45+53 | MFG-2 |

**Irish Air Corps**
Airtech CN235MPA
   Persuader | 252/7 | Maritime Sqn

**Israeli Air Force**
KC-130H Hercules | 545 | 103 Sqn

**Italian Air Force**
AS-61R/HH-3F Pelican | MM81349/15-37 | 15 Stormo/83 Centro SAR
Br1150 Atlantic | MM40123/30-10 | 30 Stormo/86 Gruppo
F-104S/ASA Starfighter | MM6704/5-44 | 5 Stormo/23 Gruppo
| MM6920/5-35 | 5 Stormo/23 Gruppo

**Royal Jordanian Air Force**
C-130H Hercules | 347 *Guts Airline* | 3 Sqn

**Royal Netherlands Air Force**
Agusta-Bell AB-412SP | R-01 | SAR Vlucht
Alouette III | A-350 | 302 Sqn
C-130H-30 Hercules | G-273 | 334 Sqn *IFOR markings*
| *Ben Swagerman* |
F-16A(R) Fighting Falcon | J-633 | 306 Sqn
F-16B Fighting Falcon | J-066 | 311 Sqn
| J-655 | 323 Sqn
| J-209 | 322 Sqn
Fokker 60U | U-04 | 334 Sqn
McDonnell Douglas | T-264 | 334 Sqn
  KDC-10 | *Prins Bernhard* |
MBB BO105CB | B-68 | 299 Sqn

**North Atlantic Treaty Organization**
Boeing 707-329C | LX-N20198 | NAEWF
E-3A AWACS | LX-N90449 | NAEWF

**Royal Norwegian Air Force**
F-5B Freedom Fighter | 136 | 336 Skv
| 243 | 336 Skv
P-3N Orion | 154576/4576 | 333 Skv

**Royal Air Force of Oman**
C-130H Hercules | 502 | 4 Sqn

**Portuguese Air Force**
SA330C Puma | 19504 | 751 Esq

**Russian Air Force**
Antonov An-72A *Coaler* | RA-72972 | VVS Transport Aviation

**Russian Navy**
Ilyushin Il-38 *May* | 22 red (11006) |
| RA-54621 | Ostrov Training Regt

**Slovak Air Force**
Antonov An-12BP *Cub* | 2209 (2209) | 32 ZmDK/1 Letka
MiG-29UB *Fulcrum* | 1303 |
| (N50903028113) | 31 SLK/1 Letka

**South African Air Force**
C-130B Hercules | 401 | 28 Sqn

**Spanish Air Force**
Airtech CN235M-100 | T19B-12/35-30 | Ala 35/352 Esc
F-27M-400MPA
  Friendship | D2-01/802-10 | 802 Esc
RF-4C Phantom II | CR12-55/12-64 | Ala 12/123 Esc

**Swedish Air Force**
AJSH-37 Viggen | 37908/81 | 2/F15
AS332M-1/Hkp10
  Super Puma | 10412/89 | F15/Hkpgrp
C-130E/Tp84 Hercules | 84001/841 | F7

**Swedish Army**
MBB BO105CB/Hkp9 | 09218/18 | 2/AF1
Agusta-Bell
  AB412HP/Hkp11 | 11333/33 *Gina* | 3/AF1

**Air Force of the Ukraine**
Ilyushin Il-76MD *Candid* | UR-78820 | 243 OSAP
Sukhoi Su-27A *Flanker* | 48 (36911014401) | 831 IAP

**United States Air Force**
A-10A Thunderbolt II | 81-0952/SP | 52 FW/81 FS *52 FW*
| 82-0650/SP | 52 FW/81 FS
AC-130U Hercules | 90-0166 | 16 SOW/4 SOS
| *Hellraiser* |
B-1B Lancer | 86-0111/EL | 28 BW/37 BS
| *Dakota Lightning* |
B-52H Stratofortress | 60-0017/LA | 2 BW/11 BS
| 60-0035/LA | 2 BW/11 BS
Boeing RC-135U | 64-14847/OF | 55 Wg/38 RS
C-5B Galaxy | 87-0027 | 436 AW/3 AS
C-17A Globemaster III | 94-0067 | 437 AW/17 AS
C-21A Learjet | 84-0085 | 86 AW/76 AS
| 84-0068 | 7005 ABS/HQ USEUCOM
C-130E Hercules | 64-18240/RS | 86 AW/37 AS
C-130H Hercules | 90-1792/OH | 179 AW/164 AS,
| *Spirit of Ontario* | OH ANG
| 85-0039/MX | 908 AG/357 AS, AFRes
| 93-7312/CR | 302 AW/731 AS, AFRes
| *Spirit of Summit 38* |
C-141B Starlifter | 65-0245 | 452 AMW/730 AS, AFRes
| 67-0029 | 164 AW/155 AS, TN ANG
EC-130E Hercules | 63-7828 | 193 SOW/193 SOS,
| | PA ANG
F-15C Eagle | 86-0167/LN | 48 FW/493 FS
| 86-0175/LN | 48 FW/493 FS
F-16C Fighting Falcon | 88-0526/AV | 31 FW/555 FS
| 89-2039/AV | 31 FW/555 FS
| 92-3918/SP | 52 FW/23 FS
F-16D Fighting Falcon | 91-0474/SP | 52 FW/23 FS
HC-130H(N) Hercules | 88-2102 | 106 RQW/102 RQS,
| | NY ANG
HH-60G Pavehawk | 89-26206/IS | 85 Wg/56 RQS
KC-10A Extender | 85-0034 | 305 AMW/2 ARS
KC-135E Stratotanker | 57-1479 | 452 AMW/336 ARS,
| *Dark Horse* | AFRes
| 59-1479 | 171 ARW/146 ARS,
| *Miss Behavin* | PA ANG
KC-135R Stratotanker | 63-8023/D | 100 ARW/351 ARS
| *Wabash Cannonball* |
| 60-0367 | 121 ARW/166 ARS,
| | OH ANG
| 64-14839 | 107 ARG/136 ARS,
| *Maid of the Mist* | NY ANG
| 61-0272 | 434 ARW/72 ARS, AFRes
MC-130H Hercules | 87-0023 | 352 SOG/7 SOS

**United States Army**
AH-64A Apache | 86-8950 | 6-6 Cav Regt

## United States Marine Corps

| | | |
|---|---|---|
| KC-130F Hercules | 149803/GR | VMGRT-253 |
| KC-130R Hercules | 160015/QB | VMGR-352 |

## United States Navy

| | | |
|---|---|---|
| P-3C Orion | 158916/LL-30 | VP-30 |
| | 160612/LY | VP-92 |
| UC-12M Super King Air | 163840/8G | NAF Mildenhall |

## Civilian

### New Zealand
Micro Aviation

| | | |
|---|---|---|
| B22S Bantam | ZK-TII | Aviation Quality Svcs |

### Russia

| | | |
|---|---|---|
| Beriev A-40 *Mermaid* | 378 red | Beriev Design Bureau |

### Sweden

| | | |
|---|---|---|
| CASA C212 Aviocar | SE-IVF/585 | Swedish Coastguard |

### Switzerland

| | | |
|---|---|---|
| Cessna 340A | HB-LPK | Bruno Stocker |

### United Kingdom

| | | |
|---|---|---|
| BN-2A-26 Islander | G-BCEN | Atlantic Air Transport/ HM Coastguard [Sat only] |
| C-47B Dakota | G-AMYJ | Air Atlantique MPCU |
| Canberra TT18 | WJ680/CT (G-BURM) | Mitchell Aircraft Ltd |
| Cessna 404 | G-TASK | Air Atlantique MPCU |
| Dornier 228-200 | G-OMAF | FR Aviation |
| Mignet HM1000 Balerit | G-MYDZ | Fleaplanes UK Ltd |
| PA-23 Apache 160 | G-BEXO | G R Manley |
| PA-28 Cherokee 140 | G-FIAT | RAFBF Enterprises |
| PA-28-236 Dakota | G-FRGN | Fregon Aviation Ltd |
| Whirlwind HAR10 | XJ729 (G-BVGE) | Austen Associates |

## HOT-AIR BALLOONS, INFLATED ON BOTH SHOW DAYS (SOUTH SIDE):

| | | |
|---|---|---|
| Cameron A-120 | G-VIKY | David Pennell |
| Cameron N-31 | G-BVFB | Bath City Council |
| Cameron N-77 | G-MITS | Mitsubishi Motors |
| Cameron N-90 | G-STRM | Royal Mail Streamline |
| | G-DRYS | J Barbour & Sons Ltd |
| | G-BTFU | Wickers World/Maltesers |
| | G-SRVO | Servo Connectors |
| Cameron N-105 | G-BWSU | |
| | G-NPNP | Air 2 Air/National Power |
| Cameron O-77 | G-BSEV | UK Transplant Co-ordinators Assoc |
| Cameron 0-90 | G-BSSO | R & J Hatton |
| Cameron O-105 | G-BWEW | Flying Pictures/Unipart |
| Cameron Fire 90 SS | G-BVYJ | Chubb Fire Ltd |
| Cameron Hopper Servo 30 SS | G-OSVO | Servo Connectors |
| Cameron Mug 90 SS | G-RMUG | Nestle |
| Cameron Pylon 80 SS | G-PYLN | Air 2 Air/National Power |
| Cameron TV-80 SS | G-SEUK | Flying Pictures/Samsung |
| Cameron V-77 | G-BTIX | S A Simington |
| Colt 77A | G-SGAS | Shell Gas South West |
| | G-BTVH | D & L Close |
| Colt 90A | G-JNNB | Justerini & Brooks Ltd |
| Colt Flying Bottle SS | G-JANB | Justerini & Brooks Ltd |

| | | |
|---|---|---|
| Colt Flying Drinks Can SS | G-BVIO | Flying Pictures/Budweiser |
| Lindstrand LBL-90A | G-BVZT | Bowyer's Pork Farms |
| Lindstrand LBL-105A | G-BWRZ | Flying Pictures/Rover |
| | G-OAER | |
| Sky 120-24 | G-BWPF | Computer Aid Services |
| Ultramagic M-77 | G-DWPH | Ultramagic UK |

## AIRCRAFT ON FLIGHTLINES (NORTH SIDE OF AIRFIELD):

### Royal Air Force

| | | |
|---|---|---|
| Dakota C3 | ZA947/YS-DM | Battle of Britain Memorial Flight |
| Harrier GR1 | XV279 (8566M) | RAF Wittering [Hangar 1200] |
| Harrier GR7 | ZD461/51 | HOCU/20(R) Sqn |
| | ZD463 | HOCU/20(R) Sqn |
| | ZD345/12 | HOCU/20(R) Sqn |
| | ZD404/33 | HOCU/20(R) Sqn |
| | ZG471/61 | 1 Sqn |
| | ZD465/55 | 1 Sqn |
| | ZD462/52 | 1 Sqn |
| | ZD470/60 | 1 Sqn |
| | ZD376/24 | 3 Sqn |
| | ZG512/83 | 4 Sqn |
| | ZG858/90 | 4 Sqn |
| Harrier T10 | ZH660/P | HOCU/20(R) Sqn |
| | ZH665/S | HOCU/20(R) Sqn |
| | ZH657/XX | HOCU/20(R) Sqn |
| Hawk T1 | XX235 | 4 FTS/74(R) Sqn |
| | XX244 | 4 FTS/74(R) Sqn |
| Hercules C1 | XV292 | LTW |
| | XV210 | LTW |
| | XV297 *# | LTW [*Falcons* support] |
| Hurricane IIC | PZ865/J | Battle of Britain Memorial Flight |
| Jaguar GR1A | XZ108/A | 16(R) Sqn |
| Lancaster BI | PA474/WS-J *City of Lincoln* | Battle of Britain Memorial Flight |
| Spitfire FIIA | P7350/YT-F *Enniskillen* | Battle of Britain Memorial Flight |
| Tornado GR1 | ZA321/B-58 | TTTE/S Sqn |
| Wessex HC2 | XR508/B | 60 Sqn |

### Royal Navy

| | | |
|---|---|---|
| Sea Harrier FA2 | ZH798/122 | 800 NAS |

### Army Air Corps

| | | |
|---|---|---|
| Gazelle AH1 | XW897/Z | 670 Sqn *Blue Eagles* |
| | ZA777/B | 670 Sqn *Blue Eagles* |
| | XZ317/R | 670 Sqn *Blue Eagles* |
| | XX385/X | 670 Sqn *Blue Eagles* |
| Lynx AH7 | XZ175/Z | 671 Sqn *Blue Eagles* |
| | XZ641/G | 671 Sqn *Blue Eagles* |

### Czech Air Force

| | | |
|---|---|---|
| MiG-21UM *Mongol* | 3756 (516937056) | LZO *Stress Team* |
| Mil Mi-24V *Hind* | 0702 (730702) | 331.vrlt/33.zVL *Skupina Mi-24* |
| | 0703 (730703) | 331.vrlt/33.zVL *Skupina Mi-24* |
| | 0710 (730710) | 331.vrlt/33.zVL *Skupina Mi-24* |

**French Air Force**

| Alpha Jet E | E141/1 (F-TERA) | *Patrouille de France* |
| | E89/2 (F-TERE) | *Patrouille de France* |
| | E140/3 (F-TERD) | *Patrouille de France* |
| | E104/4 (F-TERB) | *Patrouille de France* |
| | E173/5 (F-TERP) | *Patrouille de France* |
| | E105/6 (F-TERF) | *Patrouille de France* |
| | E97/7 (F-TERL) | *Patrouille de France* |
| | E37/8 (F-TERI) | *Patrouille de France* |
| | E106/9 (F-TERJ) | *Patrouille de France* |
| | E23/0 (F-TERO) | *Patrouille de France* |
| Jaguar E | E37/7-PQ | EC 02.007 |
| | E21/7-PM | EC 02.007 |
| | E19/7-PN | EC 02.007 |
| Transall C-160R | R13 (F-RAMH) | ET 01.061 [*UN markings*] |

**German Air Force**

| F-4F Phantom II | 37+78 | JG-71 |
| Tornado IDS | 44+92 | JBG-38 |
| | 43+25/G-75 | TTTE/A Sqn |

**German Navy**

| Tornado IDS | 45+59 | MFG-2 |

**Italian Air Force**

| Aeritalia G222 | MM62121/46-86 | RSV/311 Gruppo (on loan) |

**Royal Malaysian Air Force**

| C-130H-MP Hercules | M30-07 | 4 Sqn |

**Royal Netherlands Air Force**

| F-16A Fighting Falcon | J-508 | 306 & 311 Sqns |
| | J-511 | 306 Sqn |
| F-27-100 Friendship | C-2 | 334 Sqn |
| Pilatus PC-7 Turbotrainer | L-03 | EMVO |
| | L-07 | EMVO |

**Royal Netherlands Navy**

| P-3C-II Orion | 305 | 321 Sqn/MARPAT |
| SH-14D Lynx | 282 | 860 Sqn |

**Slovak Air Force**

| MiG-29A *Fulcrum* | 6829 (36068) | 31 SLK/1 Letka |

**Swedish Air Force**

| SAAB 105/Sk60 | 60033/1 | F5 *Team 60* |
| | 60096/2 | F5 *Team 60* |
| | 60061/3 | F5 *Team 60* |
| | 60125/4 | F5 *Team 60* |
| | 60098/5 | F5 *Team 60* |
| | 60139/6 | F5 *Team 60* |
| | 60062/7 | F5 *Team 60* |
| | 60117/117 | F5 |

**Swiss Air Force**

| F-5E Tiger II | J-3081 | *Patrouille Suisse* |
| | J-3090 | *Patrouille Suisse* |
| | J-3083 | *Patrouille Suisse* |
| | J-3084 | *Patrouille Suisse* |
| | J-3085 | *Patrouille Suisse* |
| | J-3087 | *Patrouille Suisse* |
| | J-3091 | *Patrouille Suisse* |

**Turkish Air Force**

| NF-5A Freedom Fighter | 3051/1 | *Turkish Stars* |
| | 3039/2 | *Turkish Stars* |
| | 3015/3 | *Turkish Stars* |
| | 3022/4 | *Turkish Stars* |
| | 3066/5 | *Turkish Stars* |
| | 3036/6 | *Turkish Stars* |
| | 3027/7 | *Turkish Stars* |
| | 3055/8 | *Turkish Stars* |
| NF-5B Freedom Fighter | 4005/0 | *Turkish Stars* |

**Air Force of the Ukraine**

| Sukhoi Su-27A *Flanker* | 57 (36911031411) | 831 IAP |

**United States Air Force**

| B-1B Lancer | 85-0084/EL | 28 BW/37 BS |
| | *Brute Force* | |

**Civilian**

| Extra EA300 | JY-RNA | *Royal Jordanian Falcons* |
| | JY-RND | *Royal Jordanian Falcons* |
| | JY-RNE | *Royal Jordanian Falcons* |
| | JY-RNF | *Royal Jordanian Falcons* |
| AS355F-1 Twin Squirrel | G-PASE | Police Aviation Services |
| Extra EA300 | G-HIII | Firebird Aerobatics |
| | | *Rover Team* |
| | G-SIII | Firebird Aerobatics |
| | | *Rover Team* |
| Jet Provost T5P | G-VIVM | *Transair Display Team* |
| Jet Provost T5A | G-BWEB | *Transair Display Team* |
| MBB BO105DBS/4 | G-PASG | Police Aviation Services |
| Spitfire LFIXB | MH434/ZD-B | Old Flying Machine Co |
| | *Mylcraine* | |
| Vickers FB27A Vimy IV | *G-EAOU* (NX71MY) | Green Co (UK) Ltd |
| | | (replica) |
| WSK-PZL | | |
| Antonov An-2R *Colt* | HA-MEP | AeroSuperbatics Ltd |

**AIRCRAFT IN THE FLYING DISPLAY ONLY *(DID NOT LAND)*:**

**Royal Air Force**

| Hawk T1/T1A | XX233 | RAF *Red Arrows* |
| | XX237 | RAF *Red Arrows* |
| | XX307 | RAF *Red Arrows* |
| | XX227 | RAF *Red Arrows* |
| | XX252 | RAF *Red Arrows* |
| | XX253 | RAF *Red Arrows* |
| | XX260 | RAF *Red Arrows* |
| | XX266 | RAF *Red Arrows* |
| | XX306 | RAF *Red Arrows* |
| Hercules C1 | XV297 *# | RAF LTW |
| | | [*Falcons* support] |
| Nimrod MR2 | XV229 * | RAF 206 Sqn/Kinloss Wing |
| | XV227 ** | RAF 120 Sqn/Kinloss Wing |

**Royal Navy**

| Swordfish II | LS326/L2 * | RN Historic Flight |
| | W5856/A2A | RN Historic Flight |

**Ministry of Defence (Procurement Executive)**

| Comet 4C | XS235 *Canopus* | MoD(PE) DTEO |
| | | A&EC/HATS |

# AIRCRAFT CHECKLIST

**Civilian**

*Great Britain*

| | | | |
|---|---|---|---|
| DH100 Vampire FB6 | *109 (G-BVPO)* | RJAF Historic Flt/ RV Aviation | |
| DH115 Vampire T55 | *209 (G-BVLM)* ** | RJAF Historic Flt/ RV Aviation | |
| Hunter F58 | *843/H (G-BWKA)* | RJAF Historic Flt/ RV Aviation | |
| Hunter T7 | *800/F (G-BOOM)* ** | RJAF Historic Flt/ RV Aviation | |
| Super Stearman A75N-1 | N707TJ | *Cadbury's Crunchie Flying Circus* | |
| Super Stearman PT-13D | N5057V | *Cadbury's Crunchie Flying Circus* | |

**ADDITIONAL VISITING, SUPPORT AND CHARTER AIRCRAFT (17-22 JULY):**

**Wednesday 17th July**

| | | |
|---|---|---|
| Comet 4C | XS235 *Canopus* | MoD(PE) DTEO A&EC/HATS |
| Gazelle AH1 | XX405/C1 | AAC 670 Sqn *Blue Eagles* |
| Hawk T1A | XX335/CD | RAF 100 Sqn |
| Transall C-160D | 028/12-028 | Turkish AF 12 HUAUS/221 Filo |
| | 032/12-032 | Turkish AF 12 HUAUS/221 Filo |

**Thursday 18th July**

| | | |
|---|---|---|
| BAe 125 CC3 | ZD620 | RAF 32(The Royal) Sqn |
| Beech Super King Air 350 | HB-GII | Swiss AF VIP Flight |
| Chipmunk T10 | WP962/C | RAF *Chipmunks Around The World* |
| | WP833/H | RAF *Chipmunks Around The World* |
| Comet 4C | XS235 | MoD(PE) DTEO A&EC/HATS |
| Extra EA300 | G-SIII | Firebird Aerobatics |
| Harrier T10 | ZH663/Q | RAF HOCU/20(R) Sqn |
| Hawk T1 | XX235 | RAF 4 FTS/74(R) Sqn |
| Hercules C1 | XV210 | RAF LTW |
| | XV292 | RAF LTW |
| | XV293 | RAF LTW |
| Jet Provost T4 (composite) fuselage | XS180 (8238M) | BDRT [for ES exercise] |
| Learjet 35A | T-781 | Swiss AF VIP Flight |
| Lynx AH7 | XZ175/Z | AAC 671 Sqn *Blue Eagles* |

**Friday 19th July**

| | | |
|---|---|---|
| BAC 1-11/479FU | ZE432 | MoD(PE) ETPS |
| Cessna 550 Citation II | G-BFRM | Marshall Aerospace |
| Hawk T1A | XX331/CK | RAF 100 Sqn/JFACSTU |
| Learjet 35A | T-781 | Swiss AF VIP Flight |
| Let L-410UVP Turbolet | 53+11 (800526) | German AF FBS/3 |
| PA-23 Aztec 250E | G-BATN | Marshall Aerospace |
| Tp102 Gulfstream IV | 102001/021 | Swedish AF F16 |
| Twin Squirrel HCC1 | ZJ140 | RAF 32(The Royal) Sqn |
| Yakovlev Yak-52 | 31 (RA-9111311) | Peter Scandrett |

**Saturday 20th July**

| | | |
|---|---|---|
| BAe 125 CC3 | ZE395 | RAF 32(The Royal) Sqn |
| Beech 200 Super King Air | N7775 | Total Shure |
| C-47A Dakota 3 | G-DAKK | South Coast Airways |
| C-47B Dakota 4 | G-AMPZ | Air Atlantique |

| | | |
|---|---|---|
| Cessna 210M Centurion II | G-BVZM | Zone Travel Ltd |
| Cessna 441 Conquest II | G-FRAX | FR Aviation |
| Cessna 550 Citation II | G-BFRM | Marshall Aerospace |
| Concorde 102 | G-BOAB | British Airways |
| DH84 Dragon | EI-ABI *Iolar* | Aer Lingus |
| Douglas DC-4 | ZS-NUR/PH-DDS | Dutch Dakota Association |
| Fairchild SA227AC Metro III | G-BUKA | Atlantic Airways |
| Gazelle HT3 | ZB627/A | RAF 2 FTS |
| Hercules C3 | XV190 | RAF LTW |
| PA-23 Aztec 250E | G-BATN | Marshall Aerospace |
| PA-28-151 Warrior | G-CPTM | T Mackay & C Pollett |
| PA-32 Cherokee Six 300 | G-BKEK | S W Turley |
| SAAB 340B | PH-KSM *Malmoe* | KLM CityHopper |
| Shorts 360-100 | G-OJSY | BAC Express |
| | G-ZAPG | Titan Airways |
| Sikorsky S-76B | G-BTLA | Falcon of Friendship |
| SOCATA TBM700 | 95/65-XH | French AF ETEC 02.065 |
| UH-60L Blackhawk | 95-26641 | US Army 6-6 Cav Regt |
| Yakovlev Yak-52 | 31 (RA-9111311) | Peter Scandrett |

**Sunday 21 July**

| | | |
|---|---|---|
| AS355F-1 Twin Squirrel | G-OILX | McAlpine Helicopters |
| BAe 146 CC2 | ZE702 | RAF 32(The Royal) Sqn |
| C-47A Dakota 3 | G-DAKK | South Coast Airways |
| C-47B Dakota 4 | G-AMPZ | Air Atlantique |
| Cessna 441 Conquest II | G-FRAX | FR Aviation |
| Chipmunk T10 | WP833/H | RAF *Chipmunks Around The World* |
| | WP962/C | RAF *Chipmunks Around The World* |
| Fairchild SA227AC Metro III | G-BUKA | Atlantic Airways |
| Gazelle HT3 | ZB627/A | RAF 2 FTS |
| Hercules C3 | XV190 | RAF LTW |
| Jetstream T1 | XX492/A | RAF 3 FTS/45(R) Sqn [support for Chipmunks] |
| PA-28-140 Cherokee Cruiser | G-BCGI | A Dodd |
| PA-28-161 Warrior II | G-WARR | RAF Halton Aeroplane Club |
| PA-32 Cherokee Six 300 | G-BKEK | S W Turley |
| Shorts 360-100 | G-ZAPG | Titan Airways |
| Sikorsky S-76A-II Plus | G-BJGX | Bristow Helicopters |
| Sikorsky S-76B | G-BTLA | Falcon of Friendship |

**Monday 22 July**

| | | |
|---|---|---|
| BAC 1-11/479FU | ZE432 | MoD(PE) ETPS |
| Beech Super King Air 350 | HB-GII | Swiss AF VIP Flight |
| Learjet 35A | T-781 | Swiss AF VIP Flight |
| PA-31 Navajo | ZF622 | DTEO, Boscombe Down |
| Sikorsky CH-53G | 85+08 | German Army HFR-35 |
| Transall C-160D | 035/12-035 | Turkish AF 12 HUAUS/ 221 Filo |
| | 033/12-033 | Turkish AF 12 HUAUS/ 221 Filo |

**LEGEND**

\* Present on Saturday 20th July only
\*\* Present on Sunday 21st July only
\*# Landed on Sunday only

# RAF BENEVOLENT FUND ENTERPRISES PUBLICATIONS

Titles available in this series:

## 01. INTERNATIONAL AIR TATTOO 93
The world's largest military air show
ISBN 0-9516581-4-X

## 02. MIGHTY HERCULES
The first four decades
ISBN 0-9516581-6-6

## 03. INTERNATIONAL AIR TATTOO 94
The best in military aviation
ISBN 0-9516581-7-4

## 04. ROYAL AIR FORCE ALMANAC 1995
A directory of the RAF
ISBN 0-9516581-8-2

## 05. THE REAL AVIATION ENTHUSIAST II
An amusing look at the REAL aviation buff
ISBN 0-9516581-9-0

## 06. PROUD HERITAGE
Pictorial history of British Aerospace
ISBN 1-899808-10-8

## 07. HAWK COMES OF AGE
The world's most successful jet trainer
ISBN 1-899808-00-0

## 08. INTERNATIONAL AIR TATTOO 95
The spectacular Victory Airshow
ISBN 1-899808-15-9

## 09. HARRIER – THE VERTICAL REALITY
Tracing 30 years of development
of this unique aircraft
ISBN 1-899808-40-X

Also available: the special edition
**BRACE BY WIRE TO FLY-BY-WIRE**
Celebrating the 75th Anniversary of the Royal Air Force Benevolent Fund.
This magnificent book is a tribute to the 75-year history of both the Fund and the Royal Air Force.
Fine colour prints by leading aviation artists depict individual years of RAF service, each faced by
informative text appropriate to that year.
ISBN 0-9516581-3-1 Hardback – 168pp, sturdy slipcase

These books are available from
RAF Benevolent Fund Enterprises Publishing,
Building 15, RAF Fairford, Glos GL7 4DL, England.
Tel: 01285 713300 Fax: 01285 713268.

Prices and postage rates available on application.

**The Royal Air Force Benevolent Fund thanks IMPERIAL TOBACCO LIMITED
for its support of the Fund over 25 years.**